Transcendent Love
A Metaphysical Perspective

PRISCILA PERALES

First Edition

ISBN: 0692937730
ISBN 13: 9780692937730
Library of Congress Control Number: 2017918038
Priscila Perales, Miami, FL

I want to dedicate my inspiration to *you* for being an intricate part of my existence.

TABLE OF CONTENTS

Attention, please!

If you associate the word "God" with religion and aren't religious, I don't want to lose you here. Spirituality is *not* exclusively defined as religion, so you can call the ethereal whatever suits your beliefs best: God, the divine, your higher self, the universe, Holy Spirit, spirit, collective consciousness, Buddha, Allah, divine wisdom, energy, cosmos, universal intelligence, force, source, Christ, and so on. Among these are some of the terms I will be using throughout the book to refer to the source of our faith where all pure love and wisdom emanate from.

REAL LOVE

To love or not to love—that is the question. I could say love is the creative energy that our universe emanates from, but even this definition falls short of the complexity that love is. Love is our essence, and it is transcendent. Love is tolerant and good-willed. Love is found in balance and is oftentimes misunderstood. People think they can love too much, but loving too much can throw us off into obsession and attachments that aren't loving at all. Every extreme can be unhealthy, and in this life, you're given the free will to make a left, make a right, or stay centered. Love is in the center. You can't disown people, but you can't possess them either. Love tolerates our differences and always means others well. Love is the art of dictating your feelings and your ego when they try to plague you with dread so that you can bring yourself back to balance. You don't love someone or something by making it all yours and overprotecting it. Clinging to people or to things is tainted by fear, and fear is *not* love. Love sits in perfect stillness and allows things to come and go, to rise and fall, to ebb and flow in surrender mode. Love does not take sides either. It accepts everything and everyone as perfect parts of the principal equation that sums up our entire existence. You can't love one party and hate another, because love is not found at the end of the spectrum. Accepting both parties for what they are is real love because everything in life comes with pros and cons. Love is not found in judgment because none of us is born perfect, and passing judgment reflects our own imbalance of the heart and mind. Observing our differences without disapproval is what love truly is. I do believe that all worldly conflicts and catastrophes are essentially an expression of the collective imbalance that builds up and finds an outlet to deflate and come back to its loving center. The universe is energetic, and energy cannot be created or destroyed, so if there is a bundle of accumulated negative energy, it won't just magically disappear. Negatively charged energy will find a way to channel itself out somehow so that it can become neutral again. Life throws punches at us not to beat us up but to realign and recenter us back to where we belong. Feeling too much is just as bad as not feeling enough because the former lacks intelligence and the latter lacks compassion. Being smart enough to tell the difference and strive to stay centered is key in the game of love.

People often talk about loving versus being in love. What's the difference? A racing heart, sweaty palms, and stomach butterflies are symptoms of anxiety and desire, not symptoms of love. Two souls can have a strong attraction to each other and feel a keen desire to be next to one another, but this is not love per se. The sexual energy that is felt around another person is simply a sign that both souls are calling each other to resolve a pending karmic issue. Sex is creation, so any sexual tension marks a potential creative transformation that wants to take place between two people. Such transformation is of a spiritual nature, and the attraction is born out of karmic debt. "Karma" is a misunderstood word. It is not just leftover stuff from the past. When we encounter karmic relationships, we encounter growth opportunities to transform and transmute pain into enlightenment. It has nothing to do with the past or the future because only now exists. It has nothing to do with separate entities, past-life aggressors, or soul mates. In the end, we are all one eternal consciousness, one unified spirit. All the karma we resolve helps us become more compassionate and aware of our connection to others and of our true loving essence. People come and go, and the length of their stay depends on how fast we learn the lessons they come to teach us. Some people stay throughout our lives, and it simply means they are meant to serve our purpose indefinitely—and so we call them soul mates—but the truth is, we are all one soul, and we are meant to love everyone equally. You can feel a greater attraction to someone, but attraction does not define love. Love is something we are made of and that we can feel for everyone whether we are attracted to them or not. Love is so pure and perfect that we cannot fall out of love either. We may lose interest and attraction for another person, but this has nothing to do with love. The one that falls out of love is our ego, not our spirit. As soon as we were born into our physical bodies, we became dual beings that took on the arduous task of having to discern between ego and spirit, right and wrong, light and dark. As humans, we adopted an ego, and it is this ego that believes in separation, hate, and animosity. Ego has no regard for others and ignores the true nature of our being. When we think we stop loving someone, it is nothing more than a belief of the ego that is only focused on being loved, not on loving. Ego longs to receive, while spirit longs to give. Ego wants to change others, while spirit is fully accepting of our differences. Ego wants to understand, while spirit understands it all. Being able to balance ego and spirit is crucial if we are to truly love those around us. This does not mean that you are meant to have intimate relationships with everyone, because sex is not love. Sex is meant for us to create. Love is meant for us to transcend.

I believe the biggest tragedy is living in the pursuit of an idealistic type of love that is sold to us by romantic novels and the mass media. We close our minds and convince ourselves that love emerges from perfect physical attraction or from shared ideologies and affinities. We find it reasonable to reserve our love mostly for friends, family, and intimate partners. We choose to love only the things that make us feel good and the situations that feed our peace of mind. We tell others we love them unconditionally, but our reactions tell a different story when we punish, judge, resent, and condemn them if they act in ways that challenge us. Women hop from one relationship to another, looking for the closest resemblance to prince charming, while men are on a quest for superwoman, but even royalty and superheroes have character defects that perhaps we wouldn't be able to put up with anyway, but we still daydream and long for what we idealize as perfect. Believing that the grass is always greener on the other side has made us lose tolerance and compassion for one another. We find it easy to focus on the things that are lacking in our relationships instead of focusing on all the blessings they bring us and that are packed with hidden treasures and growth opportunities.

So what is love? Is it something we only feel for people who make us feel good about ourselves? Do we only experience love when we are supported, acknowledged, touched, and understood? What about when we are challenged, ignored, abandoned, and repulsed? Do we not have the capacity to also love all the things and people who spark negativity within us? What if we were told that the challenges these people present us with were all requested by us on a spiritual level? What if we called for them to help us develop into stronger, wiser, and more compassionate human beings? What if the only solution to our adversity is to shift our perception from that of separateness, rejection, and resentment to one of love, compassion, and unity? We need to face our aversions and make amends with them to find real love.

Yes, we are all different; the universe wouldn't have it any other way. The problem is that we resent our differences because we live under the illusion of being separate entities. We forget that everything we perceive in others is a mere projection of ourselves, so we create distance and reserve our love only for a few "fortunate ones." We are here to love each other and join forces for the evolution of our species, but to challenge each other is also part of the survival equation to transcend. Our high regards aren't always held for those who try to kick us out of our comfort zones because stepping out of our safe, cozy bubbles feels threatening, but what exactly do we fear? We fear many things. We fear having to face ourselves and discovering new truths because these might encourage us to change, and we fear change because we fear uncertainty. We fear being authentic because we're terrified of judgment and disapproval. We fear being rejected because it sparks our severe fear of abandonment. But why do we fear change? Why do we fear abandonment? We fear these simply because we forget how resourceful we are. We lost our connection to our loving source and deposited our faith on external factors. We forgot that we are made of bright, powerful light and got lost trying to find it outside of ourselves, where it is dark. It all boils down to a lack of faith in love.

Lacking faith keeps us from loving deeply and unconditionally like we are meant to.

It is impossible for us to be unloved or to be empty of love. It is not possible to be abandoned or lacking. It is our ego that feels a lack of love as only the ego believes in being an entity separate from the rest. In spirit, our souls know we are love itself, and absolutely nothing that happens externally can change that. Love is the one thing that defines us all and that we have in limitless amounts, and it is the only thing we need to thrive. This is not a New-Age statement; it is a universal law based on metaphysics. We were not born to struggle, suffer, or lack. We were born to grow into the best version of ourselves by tapping into our inner wisdom so that we can express our soul's purpose in this lifetime. The only thing keeping us from manifesting our inner bright light is fear and doubt. This bright light that shines within us is called love, and we fortunately have access to it right now. Love is the only real thing we are made of. It is love that allowed us to be conceived because it wanted to participate in making this world a better place. Our love wants to leave a mark in the physical realm, and this is why we are still breathing. Love has many names too. Some people call it God, while others call it Buddha, Christ, divine intelligence, energy, spirit, light, Allah, universe—the list goes on. We all ascribe our faith to a spiritual source that in the end is one and the same. The common denominator of all gods is that they assist us in tapping into the powerful love that we are made of because it is this very love that holds the answers to all our prayers.

Love is limitless and immeasurable. In a world where we all have the capacity to love everything and everyone to the same degree, we use our love selectively. We only love the things we like and the people we are close and intimate with, but love has little to do with sympathy and intimacy and everything to do with vulnerability. Vulnerability is powerful in that it shows the full spectrum of our being. As we become vulnerable, our true colors peak out, and this opens the way for compassion as others identify with our essence. We are all made of the same dual energy, so people are bound to identify and fall in love with those who open up their souls.

Identifying with another allows for compassion, and we fall in love with those we feel compassion for. The word "compatibility" comes from the Latin word *compatī* (to be in sympathy with). In other words, compatibility stems from compassion itself. When we are compatible with someone, it is because we have learned to love them in spite of their defects, and they can do no wrong by us because we understand none of us is perfect. Even if they act in challenging ways, we are ready to stand up for them and see beyond their wrongdoings because we love them, because we feel compassion for them. We have the capacity to develop compassion for everything and everyone because compassion is nothing more than the acknowledgment of ourselves in others. Seeing a part of us in others opens the way for bonding, and it is through bonding that we learn to love. This is why we fall in love with our blood-related families so easily! We are blood related, so we see ourselves in them through this common bond. This is also what we do when we see someone else struggling with something we have struggled with before and identify with their conflict so much that we become compassionately loving toward them. The flow of love gets blocked when we fail to see ourselves in others. We stop identifying. We forget we are connected as one and that we are nothing more than mirrors and projections of each other. We never fall out of love; we fall out of consciousness. We detach from our divine wisdom, and we experience a false separateness from the rest when we forget that we are all made of the same loving energy and come from the same loving source. We build stereotypes and become prejudiced. We forget that we are all capable of doing the same good and the same bad as others because we are all made of the same amount of light and dark. Yes, even when you witness an abominable act from another and find it easy to judge him or her as cruel, sick, or inhuman, it is important to recognize that each and every one of us is made up of the same potential. Not all of us choose to use our darkness the same way, but this does not mean we are better or worse than the rest. We are all entitled to use our free will however we please, and we all become responsible for the consequences of our actions. Divine justice is always being served, and we don't need to judge others for their mistakes or for the level of consciousness they are on as they learn their life lessons.

We all have something to work on; none of us is perfect, and this is why we are still breathing. We can't escape our physical dual nature. We are all made of black and white, right and wrong, love and fear, yin and yang. We may act and react very differently to whatever life throws at us, but we are still all created equal and have the same potential to love, help, grow, and succeed as well as the potential to hate, loathe, destroy, and stagnate. It is just a matter of choice. Those who get ahead in life and constantly experience serendipitous moments of joy and fortune have simply been the ones who have decided to choose wisely. They choose love.

Real love is best explained from a metaphysical perspective because it stems from our faith and our essence, not from our desire and physical pleasure. Real love has no ego; it is purely spiritual. It understands that it has no competition because it abounds for everyone and is everlasting. People confuse love for attachment. They think that clinging to others and wanting to own them show how much they love them, when in truth they are just grasping and getting attached. Grasping leads to fear, because the more attached we become to something or someone, the more afraid we are of losing that thing or person, and this creates much suffering. The person who is genuinely in love wants the other person to be happy no matter what, whereas the person who is attached wants the other person to make him or her happy no matter what. The attached person hangs on to people and things, believing that happiness depends on receiving another person's love. The truly loving person knows that there is nothing to cling to because the flow of life can take people and objects away from us unexpectedly, so there is no point in fearing or suffering. The flow of life is perfect, and love is never snatched from us. Love is always available to us because it stems from our hearts, not from another person's devotion. The more we cling to relationships, the more we suffer. We live in a world that believes that the biggest displays of affection are shown in wanting to own and secure another person's love, but since love is not based on possessing or sealing, we are bound to struggle in this type of bond. The purest type of love is the uninterested kind, where there is no intrigue in getting anything from the other person and where there are no hidden agendas. Real love is shared between two people who already feel complete and want to complement each other, not fix or absorb each other. Authentic love offers support, comprehension, compassion, tolerance, trust, and respect in spite of anything. Attachment conditions all forms of giving in the measure it receives. Attachment passes judgment and frets. In other words, the kind of love that sparks fear and brings suffering is *not* love.

We have a right to believe in the love we idealize. We have a right to daydream about the romantic ways we want to share our love, but we don't have a right to project our idealizations onto another person and expect them to fulfill our fantasies. In the end, we are all perfectly imperfect human beings, and the fairy-tale love we see in scripted films and novels is not a clear depiction of the love that is shared in real-life situations. In this real world, we are all struggling with something and trying to make ends meet in different areas of our lives. We wouldn't be alive if we didn't have any more challenges to face or lessons to learn and overcome. For this very reason, we must be ready to acknowledge the reality of our challenging existence, stop projecting, and start loving from a realistically compassionate stance. Unless you are ready to see the truth in people and feel the same love and respect for them in spite of their imperfections, you are bound to suffer. Real love does not want to take anything or add anything; it just wants to embrace. Real love is honest and supportive in pinpointing the truth without demoralizing. Real love will help bring you into awareness so that you can become a better person in spite of your resistance or rejection. Sometimes love is tough, but tough love does not mean hurting another person purposefully. Love feels tough only when it wants to transform us into our best version and we resist this change. In the end, the person who loves truly is the one who will stand by us in the good times and the bad and who will respect distance when distance is needed if it serves our growth and evolution.

FAITH

YOUR BIRTHRIGHT

The strength and power you are made of is truly magnificent. There is nothing you can't achieve, and this is not because you are better than others. We are all equally capable. What sets you apart is your distinct and individual life purpose, also known as your birthright. Just as we all have unique and unmatched fingerprints, each and every one of us was also born with unique and unmatched personalities, gifts, and talents. Even identical twins are born with unmatched fingerprints and end up developing different gene expressions. This comes to show how unique you are and that whatever you were born to achieve is unachievable by the rest because the rest don't even desire the exact same thing you desire, so your path is clear. Whatever you dream of and aspire to become faces absolutely no competition because just like no one else possesses your identical fingerprints, nobody else possesses the capabilities you were born with to accomplish your most ardent dreams. Yes, there will be challenges, and you will live under the illusion that many others want exactly the same thing you want. Your perception will trick you into thinking that there is only so much of anything in the world that does not suffice for everyone, so you will feel the need to snatch it from the rest before it gets snatched from you, but this is false. The only reason there's competition out there is to help us develop into the best version of ourselves and to get us to tap into our own personal strengths, weaknesses, and true desires along the way. If it weren't for competition, we would not be interested in polishing our craft, so competition is literally there to aid us in reaching our fullest potential. We have all made a pact on a spiritual level to support each other in our life purpose. Sometimes the people or situations we perceive as a competitive threat are simply there to mirror back a side of ourselves we want to get better at or a side of ourselves that we refuse to take a closer look at. All in all, we attracted those "threatening" people or circumstances because we have already subconsciously accepted that they will help us rise and overcome. Competition is a blessing, not a threat. The universe has infinite opportunities and blessings for us all.

I competed in beauty pageants for four years and always wondered why I'd be entitled to win such coveted crowns from a group of dozens of girls. We were all prepared, fit, graceful, and educated and longed for the same title. "Why me, God? Why would you give me that triumph if dozens of other girls want it so badly as well? Why would I be better suited to walk away with that victory if we are all so unique, capable, smart, and ready? What is it that will set me apart from the rest? How do I rest assured that I will win? And if I don't win, what am I supposed to learn from this if I trained for hours, studied my competition, and dealt my best cards? What are we, just puppets of fate? Is my desire to win not good enough? If we all want this so bad, why is it that just one of us gets to walk out of this victorious? If we are all perfect under your grace and we are all equally entitled to succeed and achieve, then how do you decide who wins? How does fate work?"

I had one too many sleepless nights breaking my head over this. I would go to bed countless times just days before the night of the competition trying to decipher this formula. I figured that life in general is a series of competitive contests. To get this formula right would not only help me prove myself a winner, but it would also help me for future trials and challenging events. I wanted to decode this enigma with every cell of my being. For me, beauty pageants became a life riddle, much more than just a desire to bear the Miss Mexico sash across my chest. I read countless self-empowering books and journaled away in the middle of the night, trying to find answers within me. There had to be some wise life philosophy that could help ease my mind. I found it hard to believe that life just happened to us and that we were victims of circumstance. I had a notion deep in my heart that there had to be a way of thinking or a way of living that could help me tackle life's competition in a more centered and optimistic way. Beauty pageants became perfect opportunities for me to understand the synchronicity of life.

I meticulously studied previous beauty-pageant videos and analyzed the winners. I looked for a common denominator among them because I wanted to mimic whatever it was they were doing to win. I took account of their every move on stage. I saw how the public favorite did not always win because physical beauty and aesthetics are in the eye of the beholder to begin with. Society holds a standard of beauty, and nature favors particular physical aspects over others to preserve the evolution of humankind, but it goes way beyond this in beauty contests and in life in general. Attitude is just as important, if not more. The girls who won always carried themselves differently on that raised platform. It was not only about their looks. There was something about their overall energy that set them apart. One night after much reading, studying, and journaling, I finally got it. Life is not about luck or fortune. Life is all about surrendering and confident optimism. The prettiest, tallest, or smartest girl is not always the one to walk away with the title. It is the one with the most confidence who always wins. It is all about confidence, and I'm not referring to physical confidence alone but to spiritual confidence, also known as *faith*.

My life did not take me to beauty competitions to collect crowns but rather to understand faith. I competed in five beauty pageants from 2004 to 2007, and I walked away a winner three out of five times. The two times I lost were just as valuable and necessary for my growth as the three times I won, because those losses allowed me to fully understand where I had been lacking, what triggered my insecurities, and what confidence is really based on. I came to the realization that in the end, we would all win. It was not about the crown; it was about the journey. The individual life purpose of each competitor attracted them to compete so that they could undertake very unique lessons that were necessary for their own life goals. Those lessons were just as valuable as the crown itself.

I learned that when the heart wants something, it means that it is very much entitled to have it, but sometimes what it wants is not exactly the object of our desire but rather the experience that pursuing that object will give us. In this case all of us were convinced that our hearts were burning for the same sparkling crown and the coveted national or international title, but this was only the desire of our egos. On a spiritual level, our hearts were yearning for nothing more than the experience that competing for those titles represented. We aren't always fully aware of the wise reasons of the heart. Some girls found in those competitions friendships that would forever influence their lives, others found traveling opportunities to get inspired for other life endeavors, others got from it the recognition needed to get new and more exciting professional offers, and yet others learned about hidden strengths and weaknesses that helped them become better people for their future pursuits. Every single girl took home a symbolic crown; no one walked away empty-handed. Competing alone gifted us all with different life lessons. We all dreamed about winning those crowns because we were all hungry for achievement, but in spite of the results, I guarantee you we all got what we sought. The girls who didn't win the crown didn't go home defeated even if their minds thought they did. Their souls knew best. Sometimes our minds think they know what we want, but our spirits are wiser. Whatever your soul has planned for you will always be ten times more satisfying and fulfilling than what your mind thinks is good for you, and that is your birthright. If you don't understand it now, you will later when you look back and realize that things had to happen a certain way for you to come out stronger, wiser, and happier, because from birth, you are entitled to a life of joy and fulfillment. There is always a divine purpose that wants to get you closer to love and abundance. All the experiences you participate in to follow a dream offer a stepping-stone of some sort. Even if you don't walk away with the results you sought, you will inevitably have built more character, and this is triumphant enough. Perhaps you went in looking for a crown, a gold medal, a trophy, or a coveted opportunity, and instead of attaining that, you walked away with a sharper insight, a new affinity, or new strengths or new goals to mature in other much-needed areas. If you stay faithful to the belief that your birthright is to thrive—and therefore you will get to your final destination no matter what and keep working hard toward your goals without losing your faith and optimism—life will surprise you with a much more promising version of what you mentally desire.

Faith is the ultimate virtue. Beauty contests are superficially stereotyped, but like every other competition, they are extraordinary learning experiences. Those lit-up stages were my metaphysical classrooms! Competing on those huge platforms before a biased audience and an intimidating panel of judges taught me that we are always being supported by a higher power and that this higher power always has our back. I learned that all threats are nothing more than an illusion that exists only in our perception and that we all are part of a successful dream team on a mission to support each other in becoming better human beings. When I finally understood this, I remember telling God, "I understand that you are the one who planted this wish to compete in my heart for a perfect reason, so I am ready to give my all on that stage and consider myself a winner no matter what happens. I surrender the outcome to you because whatever happens will perfectly serve my cause. I have already won in learning to trust you and your divine plan because this mind-set is the shiniest crown I could ever wear." I started to think of the other competitors as angels sent from heaven to aid me in my purpose. I even visualized angelical wings on their backs and white halos over their heads, and every time I stood next to one of them, I felt supported and uplifted! I knew that whatever the outcome, I was already a winner for feeling this way. I got a new sense of what confidence feels like, and on the night of the final competition, I was a ball of excitement and gratitude, not an ounce of fear or anxiety in me. The three times I won, I understood I had not beaten anybody else on that stage. The only thing I beat when I won was my old, limiting beliefs.

In every pageant, the thing that would set me apart from the rest of the girls competing for that crown was my faith. Yes, I dreamed of winning. I savored what it would feel like to proudly wear that crown and to be acknowledged for my efforts. I envisioned all the places I'd travel to, all the people I'd meet, all the doors that would open up, the opportunities I'd encounter, and all the things I'd learn by becoming Miss Mexico. I would get goose bumps and butterflies in my stomach when I visualized it all. I learned that the intensity and vehemence of my desire was the leading sign of how badly God wanted it for me too. From that moment on, my only duty was to hand this desire over to the universe and let it get to work. I knew that everything was already taken care of and that my only responsibility was to enjoy the ride knowing that the best outcome for me would be chosen by God. This is the real meaning of surrendering and practicing faith. The universe conspires on your behalf if you only do your part and trust the process.

Whenever you want something, constantly focusing on your intention is imperative, but learning to surrender that intention is just as crucial. Easing into the habit of surrendering can be easier when you understand that you have a birthright. We all have a birthright. All the ardent desires that excite us make up our birthright. Burning with desire to accomplish something simply means that we were born with the right to manifest it. Our goals and callings were not planted in us by accident! They are there for a divine reason. Yearning and aspiring for something is the biggest sign that the universe wants this something for us too. When we win, the whole universe wins. If we want to achieve something, it means God wants us to achieve it. We are working on behalf of the universe, so if we are still breathing, it means that we still have things to achieve. If you woke up to a beating heart this morning, it means you aren't done accomplishing yet. You still have gifts to offer to the world, even if you can't see it. Feel blessed and supported by your divine energy because you are.

LETTING GO

Loving deeply can sometimes be the excuse we use to cling to people or things. Sometimes we are not meant to keep up with relationships or circumstances that hurt us more than support us. At one point in my life, I had to learn that my idealistic way of approaching others was bringing me down more than uplifting me. I wanted to believe that everyone who is damaged was a projection of a side of me that I was neglecting and that I was meant to embrace the negativity in them and learn to perceive it as my own. I believed this was the only way to mend it and make it go away. I thought that having a heart meant that I had to accept bad people and bad situations because the power of love and surrender would bring light to their darkness, but this is not always the case. The empath in me tried to identify with other people's conflictive ways. I told myself, "They are mirrors! They are simply reflecting back a side of me that needs to heal! If I get closer and shower them with love, I will heal it all." Yes, love reigns, and we are meant to accept people for who they are in spite of their defects because we are all on a journey that deserves compassion, but there is a fine line between respecting the path of another and allowing his or her path to rattle your own. You want to be a smart empath, not a weak one.

You are responsible for your own light. You work on your wellness every single day, and it is up to you to feed and maintain your own well-being. Like moths to a flame, people are always attracted to the light in others, and it is your responsibility to protect your own flame. Giving in to other people's negativity and allowing them to weaken you is not empathic at all. Self-respect sets boundaries without exceptions. Sometimes we think it's our responsibility to uplift everyone around us and to digest their depression and hate, but this is a surefire way to put your own life on hold. One thing is to help kind, humble, and respectful people in need, and another very different thing is to keep trying to be there for those who are selfish, resentful, and disrespectful. Avoiding people whose dense, negative energy drains you of your own strength does *not* make you a bad person. When it comes to staying strong, sometimes we do have to be selfish, for it is the only way we can allow ourselves to let go and rise high.

When you are onto something big and have a burning desire to rise and overcome, to reach self-fulfillment, and to pursue a more promising life path, you are sure to become the target of those who lack faith or self-confidence. Your hope and efforts can make others feel inadequate, and sometimes your own blood relatives may try to pull you down with negative remarks or a hostile attitude. This does not mean that you owe them your loyalty or your love because love and loyalty are meant for those who are deserving and receptive of it. Offering your love and generosity to those who always find a way of putting you down is like handing a thief the keys to your home. Why would you let someone in whose sole purpose is to steal from you? Thieves believe that it is fair to steal because life has not been generous to them, so to take from others seems right, but they are missing the whole point, and you don't have to be their victim. Sometimes the people we love the most try to hold us back with manipulative ways or draining energy, and the worst part is that they do it subconsciously. They will tell us they love us, but their actions express the opposite. The source of love has nothing to do with genetic or familial ties. Sometimes you find the biggest love and support in people you met later in life, and you can call them family too. Love has no intention of putting you down or holding you back. Love cares and promotes. Love focuses on your well-being, not instilling fear and resentment. If a person, place, or thing keeps pulling you back to a state of negativity or stagnation, it is perfectly wise to let it go. You will know this because you will feel it. Never discredit your gut instinct. You are not paranoid. Your body can pick up on bad vibrations. If something deep inside you says something is not right about a person or situation, trust it. You don't have to force yourself to get along or embrace negativity in others to prove to yourself how compassionate you are. Your compassion is to be applied to yourself first and foremost, and being self-compassionate means surrounding yourself with loving habits, beliefs, and relationships above all.

I once had an epiphany over dinner. I had been struggling with pro-crastination and wondered why it took me so much effort to be assertive and proactive with my decisions. My entire being wanted to do so many things, but something kept holding me back. I could not consciously de-cipher it, given it was buried in my subconscious, and no matter how many times I tried to dissect it, I just could not make sense of myself. I had dreams and ideas; I felt a purpose and a calling to go a certain way. I had hopes for the future and a vision that showed me it was all possible, yet there was always a blocking energy about me that slowed me down. My body was very well manifesting this energy in different ways, and the most obvious one was in my slow digestion. One night some friends had invited us over for dinner, and our conversation led us to talk about diet and the impact food has on our emotional and spiritual bodies. When I shared that I had been dealing with chronic constipation for a long time and told everyone that I was still trying different diet choices to heal my issue, one person told me, "It is not what you eat or don't eat that you must figure out, but rather ask yourself what is it that you are not wanting to let go of." The question really struck me. Let go of? Are you kidding me? I had been sure that I was the one who let go of absolutely everything that didn't serve me. But was I? I certainly was not. From that moment on, I made it my intention to figure out exactly what it was I had to release, and I began paying close attention to my life and my choices. I soon realized that I was still clinging to my past, still trying to pay hom-age and be sweet to people who drained my energy instead of uplifting me. I thought I acted in bona fide ways when I made an effort to keep in touch with certain people, visit certain places, or act in certain ways that really never served me and had always slowed me down. The belief that

I belonged in places or in situations where I stopped belonging long ago was not giving me the stamina I needed to keep moving forward. This subconscious attachment was blocking me, and yes, my colon made sure I noticed. The body never lies.

I learned that sometimes in life you have to look out for yourself and move forward without ever looking back. Looking back makes us cling, and clinging blocks us. There is always a new and promising path that we must pursue confidently. The only way we can reach new heights is to let go of our excess baggage and travel with a light spirit, and you can't afford to bring your past along for the ride if that past of yours is plagued with negativity or stagnating energy. Your life journey should feel like a breath of fresh air, like an exciting adventure and not like a heavy burden. People, habits, get-togethers, communities, or behaviors from the past that trigger you with anxiety, low self-esteem, and grief are all things that you have a right to let go of, no matter what. You don't owe them anything at all if revisiting them sucks the life out of you. Yes, we are all made of light and darkness, and what bothers us in others is often a side of us that we refuse to accept, but this does not mean that we are to indulge in that negativity or to pat it on the back and allow it to play a predominant role in our lives. Compassion is not about allowing others to step all over you. Compassion is about treating yourself and others with love and respect and walking away in a forgiving and nonjudgmental way from those who harm you or bring you down, even if indirectly. If, for example, you witnessed your father physically hurt your mother and this episode distanced you from him, it does not mean that in forgiving him you are meant to allow him back into your life if he never changed for the better and his presence casts a shadow over you. You will always be the bigger person in forgiving him but then letting him go because in doing so you allow real love to enter your life. Real love and real success don't visit negatively charged atmospheres, so make sure you clear yours up and surround yourself with people, places, and things that inject you with love and encouragement and never the opposite.

EMBRACE THE PRESENT

If you have ever wondered what your legacy will be, you have the option to start feeling accomplished and generous right about now because fortunately, your legacy is not some distant and unattainable endeavor. Your cause is feasible right now. There's a way of being you can adopt today to get a sense of achievement and contribution. It all starts with feeling blessed with what you currently have and where you are in this moment in time. Loving and appreciating your present circumstance is the only way to activate the flow of love and prosperity into your life. At the same time, decipher what it is about your current situation that is helping you become the person that you need to become in order to get to where you want to go. Facing life in this curious and enthusiastic manner will lead you down the road to self-realization.

Despising the way your life is today ejects you from the present moment. I am not saying to not dream and to not long for things to be different, but you can't do so coming from a place of self-pity, resentment, or holding on to the illusion that you get to decide how your life will unfold. Your thoughts or ideas don't get to decide the outcome of your life. All you have the power to mentally decide for yourself is how you deal with the present moment, and your spirit will take care of the rest. You don't need to be mentally gifted or come up with bright solutions for your future, because your mind, which is also known as your ego, does not resolve things for you, even though you think it does. You attract what you feel, not what you think. It's not your thoughts that attract blessings into your life but rather the emotion that you fuel your thoughts with. Your mind won't ever come up with real solutions to your current problems. It is your spirit that will enlighten you and lead you down the path to fulfillment once you surrender your life plans and begin to appreciate and feel grateful and blessed for whatever it is you face right this moment. Accomplished people who are considered bright, clever, and ingenious aren't accomplished solely because they are mentally gifted and one of a kind. They also happen to be highly connected to their source. That's where they obtain their creativity and problem-solving skills, sometimes without even knowing it! Our source is our spirit. Spirit is the source of all universal wisdom, love, creativity, and abundance. Our spirit is the one that holds all the answers and the keys to the floodgates of prosperity, joy, and health. This is why we are told one too many times that all our answers and guidance lie within. In a moment of crisis, we lose hope and feel helpless because we think we need rescuing and for things to be different, but it is in these decisive moments when we are expected to practice our faith in our source because our spirit is mighty powerful, generous, and independent. There is no rut we can't get ourselves out of through faith and gratitude. Our source enlightens our mind. First comes spirit, and then come ideas. It is from our sense of peace and appreciation that great creativity stems out. When we tap into our source, the solutions to our problems pop up in our heads, and this is called inspiration. Inspiration is possible when we set all egos aside and tap into our wise spiritual core.

To tap into source, all you have to do is turn to the things that inspire you and step away from the things that put you down. There is so much beauty everywhere if we just pay attention. In the midst of our conflicts and adversity are countless growth opportunities to appreciate what's real and what works instead of focusing on what's broken. It is easy to get carried away by our impulses and negative emotions when we come face-to-face with challenging people or events, which is why I applaud those who master their emotions. Those who know how to control their emotions command their destinies, which is why I can confidently say that to rule the way we feel is our ultimate life purpose. Once we learn how to govern our emotions, we become sovereign people who depend on no one else to succeed in life. By making sure we keep our frequency vibrating high with positivity and gratefulness, ideas and solutions start to flow effortlessly into our minds, people offer to collaborate with us, we receive offers, we get lucky, and we learn that our only father, boss, and provider is God (spirit). All we must do is focus on what is going well in our lives, stay away from all the things and company that aren't supportive of our well-being, and get inspired. You might help others, go out for a walk or a hike to connect with nature, explore a city to capture its beauty, journal about your dreams and blessings, call your loved ones to see how they are doing, or do anything else that can activate your positive-feeling patterns. When we take proactive steps to position ourselves in a place of appreciation, our frequency is transformed, and we attract the creativity we need to get us out of a rut. This is the constant game that mind, body, and spirit are always playing. Mind (ego) will try to trick spirit (source) out of its center, and it is up to body (actions) to keep it in check! The only thing we can control to stay centered is the way we feel through the things we think. We are emotion moderators. That is our only purpose. To tone down negativity and polarize it into positivity is our principal mission in life, which is why the people we choose to hang out with and talk to, the habits we choose to adopt, the ideas we choose to believe, and the places we choose to visit are of utmost importance to the evolution of our spirit. We always have a choice.

It is so easy to feel sorry for ourselves and point the finger. We are experts in finding excuses for our lack of joy. We will justify our sorrows and blame the flawed person we live with, our stagnating current jobs, our lack of funds, our troubled upbringing, our bad luck, our perceived enemies, the mean boss who never gives us a raise, our selfish parents who make our lives miserable, our superficial society, politics, the broken economy, the unsafe world we live in, our addictions and compulsions, our disabilities, diseased bodies, and the list goes on. We never pause to consider that perhaps all that we currently face and experience is perfectly serving our purpose and that it is all meant to strengthen our character and make us wiser. Instead of complaining and victimizing ourselves, we are meant to face our perceived adversities with an open mind and learn to uncover the hidden message and powerful lessons contained in each obstacle for us. We never reflect on how our spirit chose our current reality, knowing that it holds the biggest learning opportunities that will transform us into the people we are meant to become to fulfill our life's purpose.

What would you do if I told you that what you see is what you get and that your biggest gifts will be found in learning to love everything that is a part of your present moment? What if the people you resent are there to teach you about forgiveness and compassion? What if your addiction is there to help you become permanently sober because your life mission is so huge that any trace of substance dependence gets in the way of the marvelous gift you have to offer? What if your lack of funds is there to help you stay where you are instead of escaping because life wants to train you to find your happiness within and not without? What if your obesity is a protective shield you wear because you feel threatened and encroached all the time and it is there to teach you to lovingly stand your ground once and for all, to trust life and to speak up for yourself with confidence and self-respect? What if everything you perceive as *bad* in your life is meant to teach you how to love more, forgive, be braver, and believe?

What if it is metaphysically impossible for us to love other life circumstances until we have learned to love what we currently face? The "I am going to be happy until..." condition does not exist. You will eventually find another thing to feel unhappy for. Escaping is not the solution, ever. It is the biggest tragedy to think that feeling stuck is a sign that we must escape and look for external solutions, because the solutions are always here, now, and within reach. Solutions are never far-off, challenging, unattainable, and extraordinary things that have to eject us from the life we have built thus far. We can love our current circumstances and get creative on how to achieve our heart's desires without escaping. If our desires make us resent our current journey and day-to-day responsibilities, then we better believe that those are desires of the ego and not the heart. I once told myself I wanted to be an actress and that this was my heart's calling. The idea of becoming an actress was very seductive and alluring. Being a highly creative and imaginative person, I'm constantly looking for ways to express my creativity, but back then I was too introverted and hadn't found a way to do so. When I heard actresses talk about their dynamic jobs and when I saw them become so many different personae on screen, I was charmed with the thought of pursuing acting myself. As a child I used to write my mom letters if I had something to say because I was too shy and insecure to speak up, so I thought acting would even be cathartic for me. Even when I decided that I wanted to pursue it, I was too embarrassed to admit it, probably because I was too afraid of other people's judgment. I also had a burning desire to belong, so I guarded myself of any disapproval or rejection. I grew up with a huge need to express myself and an intuition that told me I could contribute and accomplish great things, but I had no real guidance to find the ideal vocation for my talent. I also felt stuck and out of place in the city I grew up in, so I always secretly hoped to leave Monterrey when I came of age. I wanted to explore other cities, cultures, and people. Acting just seemed right because of the praise, exposure, traveling, and creative expression that it offers, so I decided in my teens that this was the way to go. I never dreamed of being a beauty queen either, but when I made up my mind about acting, I used beauty pageants as a stepping-stone to get there. I was very driven, focused, and determined, and I won enough beauty pageant titles to meet the right people and get the sponsorships required to finally leave my hometown and debut as an actress in a different country. My efforts, discipline, and sacrifice paid off. The only problem is that after only four years of acting, I began to realize that I was not happy at all. I had never really enjoyed the journey or challenges of acting. The uncertainty of where my next project would come from, the nomad lifestyle, having no control of my schedules, the long waiting hours in the dressing rooms, the subtle exploitation I experienced, the superficiality among actors, and finding it hard to establish long-term and stable relationships were just some of the reasons I ended up feeling much lonelier than when I started pursuing this career path. I thought I wanted to act, but perhaps what I really wanted was to get out of my hometown and find an outlet for my creative expression. I am grateful for the experience acting gave me because it just led me to a keener understanding of who I am and what I'm truly passionate about, but I understand now that acting was for not me. Mine is just an example of how one can get misled when idealizing a goal and confusing it for a passion. A real actress wouldn't mind doing theater in a shabby venue for the rest of her life if that is the only chance she had to act, and this was evidently never my case. If the journey you must live through to attain the goals you set for yourself feels desolate and depressing, then you are not on the right path, and it's time to press pause and redirect your focus. The pursuit of your dreams should feel like a pleasing adventure with all its ups and downs, challenges, and setbacks. You have a talent and a purpose, and there is a place for it right now in the universe of ours, so look for your perfect niche until you find it, and don't complain if you haven't found it just yet. The life you live now is perfectly meant to lead you to where you need to go, just like how acting was not right for me but led me to where I am now, and I wouldn't have it any other way. You need to cross the icky, stinky swamps sometimes to appreciate what you really love when you find it.

Sometimes we must go through the tough, not-so-pleasant situations because karma is involved, and this is perfectly normal and something to be grateful for too. Karma is not punishment; it is a learning opportunity to rise and overcome. Karma is meant to polish a side of us that is still rough and patchy, and some people straighten themselves up right away through faith and goodwill, while others take longer to get rid of their stubborn, self-destructive ways. Those who feel sorry for themselves and resent God for the way their lives are going are giving up their power. There is nothing unfortunate about your life because it is all meant to strengthen you. We all have a different purpose in this lifetime, and there is something specific about your current life circumstance that your soul has asked to experience to benefit you in some divine way. How many times have you heard the phrase "When you set an intention, don't worry about the hows, for that is up to God"? You don't have to worry about how you will accomplish your goals. The only thing you are responsible of in the midst of a challenge or setback is to moderate your emotions so that you keep yourself in a state of gratitude, faith, compassion, and patience for whatever life presents you with. It is up to you to guard your energy and surround yourself with uplifting people and engage in healthy, uplifting habits as well. The rest will follow.

Embrace your present and everything it contains. Even the people you perceive to be in your way or the situations you perceive to be blocking you from your bliss are certainly not guilty. They're simply there as instruments to show you how to practice tolerance, develop resilience, and strengthen your faith. Ultimately, it is your belief system and perseverance that will achieve the greatest miracles you've ever witnessed. It is your self-love and compassion and not your willful efforts that will pluck the weeds from your lawn. Oftentimes life is not about willpower and all about loving wisdom.

Once you've finally tapped into a constant state of gratitude and appreciation for the way your life is, things will start to fall into place, and surprises will come knocking on your door. You will finally understand how you were never in control or knew what was good for you in the first place. God has a way of surprising us when we surrender. We end up realizing how our birthright is to live happy and fulfilled, and our minds don't always know what will bring about that bliss. Our only responsibility when facing adverse moments is to stay grounded and surrounded in love, appreciation, and faith. There are no struggles going on that you can't conquer if you perceive life this way. Perception is powerful. Perception is all there is. What you see is what you get. What you focus on magnifies. Your beliefs will always prove you right. If you believe we live in an unsafe world, you will keep hearing of catastrophes. If you believe in injustice, you will be robbed. If you believe in lack, you will struggle. If you believe in animosity, you will attract hostile people into your life to prove your faith. Faith doesn't just activate blessings. Faith can feed and activate negativity too, which is why it's important to direct your faith wisely. Believe in the good, the promising, and the loving essence of all that is because the only truth is that which you perceive.

NOW IS ALL THERE IS

Life is always happening right now, and you are complete right now. There is nothing you have to become, and there is nowhere to go because you are already everywhere, and you are everything. This concept is of course confusing because it sounds like you are meant to strive for nothing and exert no effort to accomplish anything. The only reason I want to talk about the concept of the present moment is because I believe anxiety and depression stem from feeling inadequate or incomplete in the now. As soon as we wake up, we are bombarded with social media and news headlines, and we bump into people who seem to be getting a lot done. We immediately feel an urgency to keep up and compete with the world around us. We are brought up to believe that we are meant to make something meaningful of ourselves and of our lives as if we were born incomplete or insufficient. We do have a life purpose, and we are a work in progress, but the only work that is really meaningful and transcendent is that which helps us return to our source of fulfillment and contentment that lies within. When we realize that there is really nowhere to go and that magic is happening all the time, we live our lives more profoundly. What is meant to happen will happen anyway, whether you pursue it in a state of anxiety and urgency or in a state of surrender and contentment, so why not choose the latter?

Knowing that we were born with the capacity to manifest anything our souls desire is very encouraging, but it can also make people crazy. It's important to have faith that everything is already taken care of on a spiritual level, and we must support the unfolding of this truth with grace and integrity, but we must also tame our egos. The ego believes that we need to hurry, that we are incomplete, and that we are all separate entities competing for the ideal lifestyle. You wake up and get instantly overwhelmed with a to-do list that whacks up your perception and opens up a huge void you are meant to fill as you go. You suddenly bombard yourself with false expectations to feel complete again, such as today I have to exercise to lose the weight, I have to make the calls to get the job, I have to complete the job to make the money, I have to become successful to get the respect, I have to be the loving partner to get engaged, I have to get married to get the kids, I have to look good to get the praise, and I have to get busy to feel productive. From the moment we wake up, we tell ourselves we are incomplete and then wonder why we get so depressed and addicted. We use food and pills and drinks to numb ourselves out at the end of the day because no matter how hard we try, we can't seem to fill the huge void that we dug for ourselves. If you aspire to become someone or accomplish something, by all means work toward your goal, but do it because you enjoy the journey, not because you want to acquire something from it once it's done. You don't have to believe the laws of society because they are meant to drive us insane. You don't have to be a supermodel to find love, you don't have to be a wife to become a mother, you don't have to be famous to be influential, you don't have to be sexually active to enjoy intimacy, you don't have to have a hundred friends to find support, you don't have to lose weight to be admired, and you don't have to prove anything to anyone, not even to yourself. All these things that we enjoy come find us when we are ready, not the other way around, so you might as well let go of the obsession. It is all an illusion. We wake up with a hunter mentality, but we won't ever catch anything, because as soon as you have it, you will want more. The social and economic order we grew up in and the consumerist ideology we were instilled with wouldn't have us any other way. None of it is true, and it is all meant to deplete you of your worth because you suddenly need a certain number of acquisitions and are expected to complete a specific social set of rules to fit in. You don't need to accomplish anything except to be happy right now and wake up every morning feeling complete. Right now you are everything, and you have everything, and you can tap into everything you already are by sitting in stillness even if for a few minutes. When you sit in silence and focus on the gaps and on the space that is just happening all the time in the background, you will find the very essence you are made of that contains all the peace and love you are constantly pursuing outside yourself. We live under the illusion that life happens to us, but this is not the case. We are happening all the time, and whatever manifests out there in our perception field is a projection of our thoughts and feelings, so make it a habit to feel happy and complete right about now. Forget about pursuing the life of your dreams, and focus instead on tapping into it right now because it is currently accessible to you through the way you choose to feel and perceive your world in this moment. No, things don't just happen by magic, and you are not meant to get lazy and expect your life to magically align itself on its own. You must still get to work and put in the effort to manifest your dreams; it's just that our idea of effort has gotten twisted over time. The effort starts with feeling complete and excited for your life from the moment you wake up each morning. If you haven't been feeling this passion for life, you most certainly have some soul-searching to do and letting go of unreal expectations. Life is uncertain, but it is also magical, and it can surprise and bless you with way more than you ever imagined if you just start loving yourself and your routine. Surrendering does not mean becoming irresponsible. You still have to make the right choices for yourself *now* to experience a fulfilling existence, and a big chunk of it is choosing to focus on your blessings and not your voids.

Whatever makes your heart sing is what you are meant to do. You are not meant to jog three miles each day to get fit if you cringe every time you jog. Jogging is challenging enough, but you have to enjoy the challenge of it as with everything else in life. You are also not meant to want what everybody else wants. Our goals don't have to be similar to other people's goals. Fame, fortune, and material wealth are not on everyone's wish list. Some people just want to express themselves and engage in activities that make them joyful whether it be in the arts, sciences, law, medicine, engineering, sports, hospitality, fashion, literature, and the list goes on. When we feel a lack of clarity on this and sense we are wasting our time doing nothing of significance in our lives, it simply means we are disconnected from the present moment. We always have something special and valuable to do, and we are always full to the brim with gifts to hand out to the world. The person who wakes up every morning and cooks breakfast with love, helps his or her family get on with their days, has encouraging words to say to uplift others, offers a smile to people on the street, walks his or her pet and gratefully admires the passages of nature, exercises, reads books to learn something new, or journals to explore his or her thoughts and feelings is serving the world in more ways than he or she can even imagine. You never know who could have benefited from your smile, good advice, shoulder to lean on, or help and support. You don't have to be a practicing doctor or a lawyer to feel a sense of accomplishment.

The point I am trying to make is we all have a purpose, and as long as we are breathing, we are to tap into that purpose with love and dedication. Sometimes life has you in a place where you feel stuck, but I promise you that you aren't. There is always something to look forward to, even if it is your morning cup of coffee. In other words, if you change your perception of lack of purpose to one of abundance and gratefulness, God alone will guide you into doing the things that make you the happiest. You might not even know what you want right now, but by focusing on the things that currently make you twirl with excitement, you can get a good idea. Life can get tricky when we start to compare our lives to that of others. Every so often someone comes along to brag about their amazing love lives, sex lives, travels, business endeavors, partnerships, material wealth, triumphs, engagements, weddings, pregnancies, parenthood, family reunions, social gatherings, weight loss, high-end acquisitions, or other things. Suddenly we feel like we are lagging behind and start coveting that which sounds so seductive in another. The grass will always be greener on the other side, so don't fall prey to this trap. Your friend might be having more sex or driving a nicer car, but that does not mean he or she is happier. Happiness is a choice, not an acquisition. If you saw something today that made you feel like you are missing a piece of the puzzle to complete you, take it as a sign that you are being misled by your false perception. I guarantee you that right this moment, you can find something to feel completely blessed and grateful for that can make you as happy as the portrayal of happiness you just witnessed in another. People will always find something to justify their voids, so you better check yourself before you wreck yourself! I know people who live in Beverly Hills, drive Mercedes Benzes, and love their professions but are unhappy because they are alone and can't kick their addiction to food and drugs. I know people in perfect marriages with no addictions whatsoever but complain of not living in luxury and hate their jobs. What's it going to be? It is always up to you. Don't let a false perception and constant comparisons throw you off your center. Find your source of happiness right now because God knows you have it.

THE MAGIC OF SETTING INTENTIONS

A great way to tap into your purpose is to make a wish list, detach from it, and let life surprise you. I encourage you to take a pen and paper and start writing down the things you want the most, without limitations. Be specific. Don't just write down that you want your own house but also its size, location, and features. Write down everything your heart desires, leaving modesty and guilt aside. This is where you allow yourself to dream and get creative. It is a great tool to tap into your imagination to discover what it wants to come up with. Remember that if you can imagine it, you can achieve it. Many people have a hard time believing this because they get attached to a specific outcome, and when it doesn't happen, they lose faith. Many times the very thing you visualize is not exactly what you are meant to do or have, but a similar thing that gives you the same amount of joy and pride is sure to come your way. For this to happen, you must detach from the specificity of your wish list after you've jotted it down.

It is important to become aware of what you want because intention is power packed. Honoring your desires is a self-respecting thing. Not knowing how those desires will come about is perfectly normal too. You are not meant to decipher the hows. How you will move to a new city, how you will get a new job, how you will get funds for a new project, how you will get the chance to travel, how you will be discovered, how you will find the man or woman of your dreams, or how you will find your freedom is *not* up to you. This is up to God, who orchestrates your life according to perfect timing. The universe holds your best interest and has already figured it out for you. Your spirit is just waiting for you to get clear on your desires, have faith, get happy, and surrender.

Surrendering your desires is only possible through detachment. To detach is just as important as dreaming in the manifesting formula. Detachment means that you find your happiness in whatever you are doing now even before those aspirations of yours take shape and form. You must carry on living an honest life in the company of supporting people and let life surprise you. Learn to love those who are part of your life right now. Help others in whatever they are doing. Engage in activities that keep feeding your creativity and nourishing your soul. Honor your body, and keep it strong and healthy. Deliver 100 percent in your current employment, and feel grateful that it pays your current bills. Send thank-you notes. Visit a friend, or have them come visit you. Give the present moment the respect, regard, and appreciation it deserves, and expect miracles to happen.

The universe pays attention to your heart's callings, but then you must get out of its way and find activities to stay centered in the present moment. Stop expecting, start believing that whatever does happen will be perfect, and get back to living your life in a confident and self-possessed way. Taming the mind and emotions when they want to react negatively and control outcomes is what mastery is all about. I used to lament over petty things. I never felt accomplished enough in my career endeavors. I felt sorry for myself for growing up without a father. I felt jaded for using alcohol to deal with my inner turmoil. I felt awkward in reaching the thirty-year mark without marriage or kids under my belt. I was flooded with confusion as to who I was and what I was supposed to do with my life. Having support from loved ones was not enough, and I'd focus on all the things that bothered me about them and all the things they didn't do for me. I fell prey to the vicious cycle of finding excuses to justify my feeling stuck, blocked, and bored. I became good at resenting everyone and everything for my despair until one day I decided to wake up. I realized I was constantly trying to escape myself. My attitude was a recipe for disaster, but I was not doing anything to feel better either. I still stuck to the same bad habits, I still hung out with people who kept me in a stagnant mind frame, and I still compared my life to that of others and resented the world. Staying stuck and feeling sorry for myself were the very things that were keeping me from living. Absolutely nobody was to blame for the way my life was unfolding. Nobody could have done anything to make me happy because our happiness never depends on external factors. If we think we'll be happy when things or other people change, we will be forever disappointed. As soon as we get what we want, we'll be sure to find yet another reason to indulge in negativity because we ignore the fact that our true source of happiness is always within, not without. Unless we fix our self-defeating mind-set, we will never get to experience how lucky and abundant we already are, and it all starts with setting the right intentions. Intend to let go of all the energy, behavior, and people that no longer serve you once and for all. Intend to claim back the energy that does propel you to bigger and better things. Intend to focus on the now and the blessings that the present moment gifts you with. Intend to aspire for the best and work hard toward it. Intend for a journey that is enjoyable and goals that infuse you with excitement and adventure.

At some point I decided to replace my crushing negative mental chips with chips of principle and truth. For instance, I did grow up without a father figure and experienced rejection and bullying in school, *but* this only fueled my drive to overachieve, which is probably why I was such a diligent student, got scholarships in college, and won state, national, and international beauty pageants (no one bullied me after that). My mother was always working hard to raise me and my brother, so she was rarely home, *but* this helped me become more independent and brave in later years. Yes, I used to drown my insecurities with alcohol, *but* the depths that I experienced when numbing my feelings and poisoning my body helped me appreciate the clarity, sharpness, and confidence that I acquired once I decided to live in full sobriety. After four years as a beauty ambassador, I pursued acting to channel my creativity in the arts. My acting career never soared to great heights, not because I was a failure *but* because my priorities shifted and I was bold enough to take on new endeavors in search of myself. Once I partnered up with the flow of life, I became aware of all the shifts in consciousness that I began to experience. We always have the option to shift our focus and transmute our feeling patterns from deceptive ones to encouraging ones. There are no bad experiences unless we make them so in our heads. That's how powerful we are.

GET WITH THE PROGRAM

Being proactive is imperative in the path to fulfillment. Getting lazy because we trust God has got our backs is not what life is about. You must work with what you have where you are and make the best of it. When life gives you lemons, you make lemonade, right? You don't store the lemons away in a drawer, hoping to magically find a lemonade pitcher in the fridge. You don't complain that the lemons aren't the shape, size, or color you expected them to be, right? Lemons are lemons! Being a righteous person is all you need to worry about because acting with integrity builds character, and character is what ultimately takes you far in life. Doing things right, in a dignified way, such as showing respect to your work and your peers; being punctual; honoring your body; surrounding yourself with supportive, loving, and uplifting people; and focusing on what's good in your life instead of what's lacking are only a few of the things we must do to let the universe know we are ready for more blessings to manifest for us. Like Algernon Sydney once said, "God helps those who help themselves."

Yes, God will help you, the universe will provide for you, and you are taken care of, but only if you lead a bona fide life. You can't cheat yourself to succeed. If you do, you won't get true satisfaction from it anyway because you'll live with a murky consciousness. Your spirit only knows about honesty, integrity, and real effort, so trying to get ahead in life in a dishonest way misaligns you from the truth. Only when the spirit feels aligned with truth will magic start to happen. You can't cheat your soul; it knows best. You can't have dark secrets, act in self-destructive ways, wish others bad fortune, cheat people, cheat in business, disrespect your peers or your current employment, resent the status quo, or procrastinate and expect to live an extraordinary life. And I bet some of you are thinking, "For God's sake, Priscila! Are you telling me to love the people who aggravate and hurt me? To be sweet to the unjust? To happily show up every morning to the work that exploits me? To respect the politicians who rob my tax money? To come home after an exhausting and enslaving day at work and find time to honor my body? I just want a beer and a couch!" The majority of the population feels comfortable thinking this way. It is a comfort zone. It is a mind-set that does not challenge us, so we embrace and protect it. Thinking this way is quite ordinary. This is the main reason why only a few achieve the extraordinary.

What is extraordinary? Extraordinary is remarkable, exceptional, and noteworthy. People who act in remarkable ways and adopt exceptional mentalities are the people who achieve noteworthy results. We then call these people lucky, fortunate, and gifted, but they earned their fortune and activated their luck. They tapped into their spirit, found strength in their faith, understood that they were responsible for every aspect of their lives, and got with the program. No, I am not telling you to be ultrasweet to the people who aggravate you, but don't aggravate them back either. There is character and honor in respectfully walking away from a person or situation that belittles or hurts you. You don't have to strike back with violence or vengeance. Reacting in aggressive, impulsive, and disrespectful ways is immature and ignorant. No, you don't have to applaud a government that robs you, either, but when you are feeling robbed, how about you ask yourself when or where in your life are you robbing others of something or even robbing yourself? Remember that life makes sure to project back at you what you carry within. There are so many businesses that thrive amid political and economic crises, and I can safely tell you, this is not a coincidence. Nobody gets lucky; all the luck in the world is a result of good karma and good faith. Some people don't rob anyone of anything but believe they are vulnerable to thieves, so life will make sure to manifest that belief. You are only vulnerable to what you believe in, and what you believe is reflected in the things you think, say, and do, so make sure to be a person of righteous thoughts, words, and actions. Integrity, my friend. You won't know the heavy weight of the negative thoughts and actions you engage in until you free yourself of them and walk lightly.

COMPASSION

COMPASSION LEADS TO BALANCE

Compassion is the permission we give ourselves to love. To decipher how compassionate you are, just ask yourself how much love you normally give out. We aren't just randomly compatible with people, situations, or ourselves. Being compatible enough to spread our love with others is a choice. You ultimately decide who you want to pour your love out to and to what degree. This is why we take the time to get to know people so that we can find out if the connection calls for a deep love exchange, a caring friendship, or just a kind and fleeting interaction. Romance is a form of love, just as there is love in friendship too. Loving and being compatible with another person do not always mean you have to establish intimacy or get married because two souls are not always looking to bond that deeply or spend that much time together. The universe is wise, and it will plant the strongest feelings between souls that are in desperate need of balancing themselves out. Compassion is energy driven, as is everything else in the universe. We brush shoulders and cross paths with the people who subconsciously have some valuable lesson to offer us and from whom we are ready to learn something new, so our energies find each other. Sometimes the most compatible people have the most destructive relationships because they resist change and fear giving up the things that will offer them precious balance, yet they don't understand that this is why they're highly attracted to each other in the first place.

The universe is always trying to balance itself out, and balance is found in love. Either you will find someone to share your balanced love with or you will find someone who teaches you how to love again because the soul is always looking to return to love. Some people teach us how to love deeper and how to be more grateful, more faithful, tolerant, or even more genuine. The time will come when you'll fall out of balance, and life will make sure to realign you by throwing you into testing relationships to strengthen your love and faith, and not everyone withstands these trials. People are used to jumping from one relationship to another, switching lovers, friends, partners, bosses, or employees without reaching a balance first. This is the way animosity and hostility are built. People split on bad terms, force divisiveness, and walk away with an ego instead of allowing life to take its natural course. The universe is always looking out for us and guiding us to a place of love, peace, prosperity, and abundance until we decide to get in the way with our ego-driven attitudes. Blame, judgment, and disdain come to play in those who refuse the way of compassion. If you reject somebody and avoid them like the plague, you can rest assured that this person has shown up with a purpose in your life. Your spirit called them into your realm of perception to offer you a precious growth opportunity, given growth only happens from a place of balance. You don't bump into random people by mistake, and people you already know don't keep coming back into your life by accident. They are there to reflect back at you the state of your consciousness. They are nothing but fictitious characters playing out the script you wrote in your imagination about life as perceived through your own lens. If you encounter friction, judgment, or rejection, then you will have found a diamond in the rough, for every tumultuous relationship signals back at us a neglected side of ourselves. There is nothing anybody can do to hurt you. The only thing that hurts is your resistance to forgive and keep loving.

So who are we compatible with? The word "compatibility" stems from the word "compassion." In essence, we are compatible with the people who offer us the chance to practice love and kindness and whom we are ready to love and be kind to, whether it be a spouse or a colleague. In other words, we are compatible with someone when we allow ourselves to love them. Compassion is a virtue that we must constantly nurture and practice. We are not just luckily compatible with some and not with others. We ultimately decide on a subconscious level whom to be or not to be compatible with depending on how each person fits our set of beliefs. We make the choice to feel empathic toward new people, new life circumstances, or even ourselves. We aren't incompatible with people because of our differences but rather because we chose to judge them and set them apart. Incompatibility is therefore the product of rejection, and rejection happens when we refuse to see ourselves in the eyes of another.

Compassion is the biggest expression of peace because it acknowledges that we are all one and the same. We are all walking different paths of life and dealing with different struggles in the process, but we are one and the same nonetheless. We mirror back at each other our flaws and virtues. Everyone out there is an illusion whose sole purpose is to show you how deeply or shallowly you are loving. The people you butt heads with the most are the ones who are offering you a profoundly healing transformation. When we stop running away from growth and allow our hearts to fill to the brim with compassion, time stops and blessings knock on our door.

YOUR ANCESTORS MATTER

Why are some born into riches and others into poverty? What kind of a curse is it to be born diseased while others take their first breath in perfect health? How can we explain that some people are prone to addiction while others aren't? Who decided that some would be inclined to the arts and others to science? Where is the mysterious universal CEO who appointed each newborn baby with a specific religion, race, and nationality? Did God just randomly flip a coin to decide the shape and form of our physical bodies, family members, lineages, talents, and inclinations? How can we believe in justice when others seem to have it so easy in certain areas of life that we highly struggle with? Are we really doomed victims of fate, or is this all part of a perfectly crafted plan to help us strengthen our hearts, break patterns of past generations, have breakthroughs, and reach fulfillment?

How do you describe yourself? Who are you? Are you defined by your last name? Your race? Your nationality? Your social status? Your profession? Your current mood? What exactly makes up the very essence of who you are? Whomever and whatever you believe you are is true, so pondering a little on all possibilities can help you decide.

Metaphorically speaking, we were handed a welcome basket full of random ingredients when we were born, and we are expected to create the best life we can imagine with those ingredients. You might feel like you were handed an incomplete basket that needs many key components for you to be able to fulfill many of your repressed dreams, but this is not true. Your basket was filled up by your ancestors, and they made sure to leave you the precise ingredients to help you achieve great things. It is in their best interest that you do because your resolution will help dissolve karmic patterns, complete any unfinished business from the past, and improve your genes. This benefits and liberates not only your entire lineage but also your future generations and the universal collective consciousness as a whole.

Do you really think we have a life purpose that we individually came up with? Why would we randomly choose to like certain things and hate others? Nothing in our lives is a coincidence or an accident. Our ancestors achieved things that brought them much joy, accomplishment, growth, and breakthroughs, but they also made mistakes that caused them despair, pain, injustice, and blockage. When their lives on earth came to an end, they left some unfinished business, unresolved emotional wounds, frustrations, and dust for us to clear up. As the spiritual beings that we are, we chose to be born into our current lineage. We chose our current family because our spirit knows that dealing with their ancestral history and spiritual debt will help us overcome our own individual obstacles and carry out our spiritual purpose so that we can transcend. When we transcend, we help the entire universe transcend too because we are all connected in spirit. It's a universal law that we must learn our lessons or else they'll keep showing up until we learn. If our ancestors died without learning a specific life lesson, it will be turned over to us for us to master it. This is our ancestral heritage, and there's no way around it. We must live responsibly, knowing that our accomplishments in this lifetime will become universal feats that will benefit humanity as a whole because we are all one. This is why there's no real competition, struggle, or animosity anywhere. The universe wants us all to succeed because our gift to humanity is unique and benefits everyone. There is no such thing as an incomplete welcome basket at birth because it is in God's best interest that we work to evolve together.

Whatever blockages we experience are there to show us what we need to work on, but it is important to embrace our barriers with compassion.

If we perceive our challenges as curses from hell, our healing process will take forever until we learn to accept them as blessings from God. Perceiving obstacles as great opportunities for evolution is key to move forward. We must not allow our perception to be clouded by our ego's negativity because in the midst of tough situations, our ego is on a mission to betray us. Ego will tell us that we are incapable and weak. Ego will victimize us and persuade us that we are alone in our journey and that we must put our guard up against the evil world and its unfortunate events. Our biggest challenge is to control and monitor our ego and choose to follow the advice and guidance of our spirit because both ego and spirit have manifesting power. Unlike ego, our spirit will reassure us and remind us that we are made of love, that we have a divine purpose that is supported by the entire universe, and that there is nothing we can't accomplish, because all we want for ourselves are things that the entire spiritual realm wants for us too. Spirit only knows about love, compassion, abundance, health, and prosperity, while ego believes in pain, hate, conflict, strain, and misfortune. Fortunately, we have a choice, and if we choose to make use of what life throws at us with compassion instead of defensiveness, we will surely make our ancestors proud and reach our biggest potential.

There is nothing more our ancestors want than for us to succeed and break negative feeling patterns. Trust me; your clan wants to be liberated! Generations keep accumulating ancestral baggage that needs much healing and much clearing. From a spiritual plane, all your forefathers and foremothers are betting on you to make things right, to heal wounds from the past, to act in wiser ways, to spread more love, to respect your body, and to live with dignity, integrity, and faith. They are all placing their bets on you to set your boundaries, to stand for what's right, to be an example of good character, to abstain from gossip and judgment once and for all, and to always see the good in others. How many mistakes did our ancestors make because of bad judgment, lack of love, lack of faith, and lack of clarity? Many. All of a sudden, we are born with ailments we can't explain, family members we clash with, addictions we can't control, and predicaments we didn't choose, and we grow up having to figure it all out without a disclaimer or initial introduction of what was to come! Resentment builds up, and we find solace in numbing substances; we blame our past and our present, and we fear the future. Our focus ends up fixated in all the things that weaken us, and we lose sight of our strengths and purpose.

You have a choice to break free from old, limiting beliefs that have been passed down to you from previous generations. You can melt away all the fears your ancestors lived with. You can be the new crowned leader of the pack. You can set new rules, take different routes, and achieve what was considered unachievable. You were born with a clean slate and were given a limitless imagination and free will to build the life you desire. You have the choice to come up with new ways of approaching life and relate to new people who can support your vision. You are welcome to look for new opportunities in foreign lands if need be. Yes, you can pave your new way, and you don't have to look back—just don't forget where you come from. You must first learn to forgive, love, and accept your lineage and family to be able to move on to bigger and better things. Walking away with resentment, bitterness, and hate is like traveling with excess baggage. Forgiving everything and everyone from your past is essential to your new endeavors because a heavy heart can only get so far. You don't have to feel proud of the way you were brought up or the people who hurt you in the past, but you do have to understand their limitations and treat them compassionately. Honoring your origins shows maturity and magnificence. It tells the universe you took what it gave you as a learning experience to avoid making the same mistakes in the bright future you envision for yourself.

There are no perfect families out there, so you can't sit and lament not being born into a more unified, brighter, wealthier, or more loving clan. Consider yourself lucky that you were born in the first place, and remind yourself that you chose your blood to teach you what you came here to learn. If you had honest, affectionate, and involved parents, you were very lucky, and if you had dishonest, troubled, and absent parents, you were just as lucky. Your blessings and treasures are not measured in the behavior or presence of others in your life, and that is one of the key lessons you came here to learn. Many children of abusive parents grow up to become exceptionally successful role models, just as countless kids raised by loving parents never build enough character to reach their full potential. Your past does not define your present or your future, so you might as well start making amends with it. You have a right to go your own way and become independent, as this is necessary to break free from old patterns, but you have to do it compassionately. Your past will always haunt you if you don't make peace with it and let it go. Resenting your past guarantees that you'll get stuck because resentment is a form of attachment, and how can you go far in life if you are attached to your past? You may choose to disengage from some aspects of your familial archetypes, but don't pretend like they were all detrimental. We are all made of good and bad, and there is a chunk of greatness that you inherited from those genes that will help propel you to new heights. Honoring your ancestral heritage and your roots shows compassion and respect for your process, no matter how hard it was. You want your ancestor's blessings. When you move on to bigger and better things and adopt a more promising attitude, think of your ancestors and family members as the ones who gave you the opportunity to be born and achieve what they couldn't. Tell them how you will make things right now that you have been given the chance. When you heal, your whole clan will have healed. When you reach new heights, your whole lineage will throw a party in the heavens, and you will have spiritually opened new doors and windows of opportunity for your current and future generations.

Get curious about where you come from. Ask questions. Find out what patterns have been repeated over and over again so that you can learn some of the potential challenges you currently face. If you don't have this information, don't worry. The memory of your lineage history is imprinted in your subconscious mind. When we start experiencing life, all the baggage we carry from past generations becomes obvious to us in whatever physical and psychological issues we begin to face. If you notice, for instance, that you keep attracting emotionally unavailable people into your life, then you will know what your ancestors dealt with. Anything that diminishes the quality of your life experience is ancestral baggage. It is up to you to make things right by choosing to enter these dark experiences with a lit-up candle of truth and transmute it to good. You have the power to choose a different set of beliefs, act in ways that propel you to a better life, and do it all in a compassionate and loving way. You don't have to struggle. You just have to surrender; replace old, limiting beliefs with new, promising ones; and start walking in the direction of your dreams.

Once you make peace with where you come from, you can start dreaming of new possibilities. Don't fall into the trap of comparing your basket to that of the rest. You can't lament and you can't covet other realities, because everything you were born into has a divinely wise purpose. Everything you dream of becoming is perfectly achievable. If you can see it, you can have it. Consider everything you perceive in the world as a catalog of what is possible for you. If you admire certain people, it just means that you have what it takes to be at their level in your own particular way. This doesn't mean that you'll clone into your idols. You have a unique star that shines in your own unique way through your own unique talents and by your own means. Like I said before, there is not a single person out there with your same fingerprints. Not even identical twins share the same fingerprints, so why would you want to be like someone else if you have such a unique imprint of your own? The subject of your admiration is just there to show you what is possible for you and to inspire you to go polish your own diamond in the rough.

The same goes for all your perceived misfortune and conflict. Your obstacles and adversity are there to help strengthen your faith and help you build resilience. Warriors did not reach warrior status by surfing through life untouched. They fought battles and rose up victoriously. Warriors will show you their scars and tell you of the many times they had to face their fears and inner demons. We admire warriors because they beat the odds, gained strength, and became wise, but that wisdom was acquired through trial and error. Their strength and glories were earned. We all have to earn our triumphs, and we can do it either the egotistical or the spiritual way. The way of the ego can be tedious, long, and painful. The way of the spirit is compassionate and allows us to heal while we enjoy the ups and downs of the journey.

DECODING YOUR GENES

Now let's talk about genes and how they also support our purpose. Believe it or not, the gene pool of the body you were born into is absolutely perfect and meant to serve your purpose. Your physical features, including your flaws, are not in vain and will somehow lead you to a better understanding of yourself and the universe. At some point in your life, you are meant to discern the role that your body plays in your spirituality and how its very unique attributes are meant to help you tap into your God-given state of joy and delight. If you were born into a deficient, disabled, short, tall, dark, fair, strong, or weak body, this won't keep you from carrying out your purpose as long as you understand you were born with no limitations. Physical barriers are also meant to teach us about our essence and lead us to a stronger faith and self-confidence so that we can become huge sources of inspiration that serve humanity. There are old souls who easily come to terms with their physical challenges and transform them into strengths by the use of compassion and introspection. Younger souls might need to delve deeper to acquire this valuable awareness and appreciation for the first time. Whichever the case, you need wisdom to allow yourself to embrace any physical burden you resent. Wisdom allows you to see the bigger picture and take proactive steps to overcome physical barriers. We can change our genes—this is a fact—but it will take awareness that leads to compassion that leads to gratefulness that leads to optimism that leads to action that leads to healing. Most physical ailments work as divine messengers that shed light on personal issues that are crying for help. The issues that we all deal with are linked to a disconnection from our source of faith. Since all the love we seek lives within us, our bodies will always be the first one to communicate to us where we are lacking through disease, discomfort, or disharmony. We have the power to change our genes through wisdom and a compassionate approach. Becoming aware of your origins and ancestral heritage does help, as it shows us what patterns have been dealt with in our past and what we can expect in this lifetime. Our genes carry information from our lineage; they are not an accident!

If you are still breathing and having a heartbeat, this is the greatest sign that you still have great things to accomplish and way more love to give and receive than you can imagine. Some people talk about losing purpose and the fate of dying young, but God has never meant to cut our lives short. We are meant to live long and healthy lives. Why would God bless us with purposeful life and then tragically interrupt its course? Our purpose is not to die young. There is no such thing as suddenly dying because we have completed our mission or because it is God's will. God is so tremendously compassionate and loving that his will is for us to live in health, prosperity, and longevity until we decide it's time to go. Many people will protest this idea and say that none of us can control accidents, tragedies, or being at the wrong place at the wrong time. If you believe in the concept of injustice, then you will live to experience unjust suffering.

Every single dramatic experience is meant to align us in truth, not to destroy us. Sometimes our biggest purpose is to prove to ourselves how far we can go. Miracles are the product of perseverance, faith, and having the certainty that we will pull through, no matter what. Never giving up is the one thing that will bring about synchronicity for all the right elements to come together and manifest magic. The journey to reach the top of the mountain may present you with valleys, harsh weather, insect bites, and scary cliffs, but if those factors don't throw you off and you stay focused in knowing, you will get to the top in spite of it all, and then you will tap into your source of strength, accomplish amazing feats, and live to tell your story. The person battling a terminal disease, struggling with disabilities, coping with loss, or hooked on addiction is facing a valuable and divine lesson meant to liberate him or her from the chains of fear, hate, and pessimism. Your genes are not meant to limit you or end your game unless you give up on life, and that is your choice.

How do we know what we are meant to do in this lifetime? What is the homework that our ancestors left us with? It's very simple. Make a list of the things that bother you, concern you, afflict you, and scare you the most. Also make a list of the things that attract you, move you, and make you happy. All the things that we resent about our lives are meant to help us surrender, forgive, and let go. All the things that we are passionate about are meant to help us channel out the love we have to offer. We were each gifted with a different way to express our love. What is yours? Your genes know best. Our ancestors developed many skills and talents, but they also dealt with many issues, many of which they never fully resolved. All these virtues and flaws have been passed down through generations and are embedded in your genes. If you are struggling with something, it is because your past generations were not able to fully sort it out, so it is now your turn to give it a shot and get it right. The same goes for all the things you are passionate about. Your passions are a result of what your entire lineage strives for. It is a combination of desires accumulated through the ages that, if accomplished, will be highly celebrated by the entire spiritual realm that injected life into your physical body. It is your homework to excel this time around, and the best part of it all is that it just boils down to *love* and *being*. Truthfully, all you have to master is the art of loving and being in the present moment. From a place of stillness is where all your creativity will flow and where you will get your deepest sense of purpose. Your life is the greatest gift you were given to mend all conflicts, dissolve all blockages, and live with an open heart. Your greatest gift to all humankind will be to learn how to love deeply and to make the best of every step you take on this planet. This is all possible through compassion. We must develop compassion for our past, our present, and our future generations.

To make amends with our present, we must first start with ourselves. Our gene pool defines our physical bodies, which take us everywhere and allow us to get things done in this lifetime. If we don't start by accepting our bodies, it will be hard to develop a compassionate approach in life. Compassion happens when we surrender to a higher truth and trust that whatever body we were born into is perfectly capable of regenerating itself to reach new heights. Your body is indeed *perfect* because whatever your genes have gifted you with or limit you on will ultimately fuel your drive to further develop yourself in certain areas that will help you thrive. The body is constantly manifesting or channeling out our emotions and beliefs so that we take on the form of our mental and spiritual expressions. It is very common for generations to pass on their very particular ways of coping with life in general. Many customs and beliefs of a tribe leave a mark on their genetic pool which is why we inherit from our ancestors not only physical traits but personality traits as well. We are born to evolve our genes and to find new and improved ways of overcoming obstacles and amplifying our talents. Science has already proven the physical origin of many diseases and disorders, but I challenge you to dig deeper and root out the emotional and spiritual causes that have us dealing with physical impediments. For example, a person who lives with much fear and trust issues might face life in a very defensive way. The body picks up on this fearful energy and works on developing fat stores as an attempt to *protect* or *shield* the soul from external harm. Until the person learns to dissolve his or her fear first, it will become hard or practically impossible to get rid of his or her extra weight. You must dive into a deep soul search to help you figure out what your genes are trying to tell you so that you can break free and write a new story. It suffices to say that you must also take care of your body in terms of diet and movement. The work starts from within, but you must also make sure to nourish your cells and feed your body with the nutrients it needs to thrive. Body, mind, and spirit are intertwined. You can't heal one and leave the rest undernourished.

Whichever concept you hold of yourself, just keep in mind that your genes are like hunger pangs that keep you hunting for truth. If you were born sick, you will hunt for health. If you were born into a socially discriminated body, you will hunt down civil rights or a sense of equality in your heart. If you were born tall, you might be called to become a basketball idol; who knows! Genes are life compasses. Your DNA is meant to drive you to become the best version of yourself. Your imperfections should be regarded as sacred, full of purpose, and packed with meaning because nothing is in vain. If our bodies were perfect and didn't challenge us in any way, we would not be trying to come up with solutions. It is all part of a perfect plan to help us further develop self-love and kindness. It is in your best interest to improve your genes, and this is not a superficial thing to say. Having *good genes* is not about physical symmetry; it is about survival and evolution. The healthiest, strongest, and most balanced bodies will withstand harsh environments and make it through the ages. Balance and survival are our ultimate goals. I believe most of us strive to live a long and rewarding life, and we have it in us to make it happen.

LOVE YOURSELF

It all starts with you because you are the definition of love itself. Your essence is love, you come from love, and to love you will go. Your natural tendency is to love; this is why when you stray away from it, you suffer. When you misalign with your heart, your spirit feels out of place and longs to go back to its essence. You may be loved by others, but you will never feel complete until you learn to love yourself. Self-love starts from a place of surrender, compassion, and tolerance. Whatever you thought, said, or did in the past does not exist anymore. Letting go of what does not exist and welcoming new possibilities is part of the equation. Today is a new day that grants you the opportunity to start anew. You can reprogram your mind to adopt new habits and a new way of treating yourself to feel the love that attracts more love. To really love yourself is an art. Today is your canvas, and your thoughts will paint your reality. There is no one else, nothing else, and nowhere else that can offer you the love you seek unless you decide to appreciate what already is. Other people do play a huge role in our lives, but the way to handle relationships in a harmonious way is by engaging in self-loving behavior, because it all starts with you. Believe it or not, you are constantly creating your own life movie, and this includes the characters, the settings, the conflicts, and also the happy or tragic endings. You might not feel like you are in control, but you are. You control your feelings and your beliefs, and it is from these two that your whole reality stems from, so you must make sure to feel and believe in love. We may choose our reality from a conscious or a subconscious level, but we are always making a choice nonetheless.

Loving yourself requires the maintenance of body, mind, and spirit. The way you treat your body, the thoughts you choose to believe, the words you choose to express, and whether you feel separated from or merged to the world around you all play an imperative role in the way you love yourself. When you feel like a separate entity, you lose connection to your source from where everything takes life and end up looking for love outside of yourself, where it does not reside. As mentioned before, it all starts with you. You have the power and the choice to start honoring yourself through loving acts and loving concepts that pump you up to live a fulfilling life. Patting yourself on the back for your wrongdoings and living in a comfort zone won't do the trick. If you want to feel more love, doing the same thing you have been doing for years and expecting different results is obnoxious. You must get to work and reprogram yourself from within because this self-love thing is not about willpower; it is about kindness. God won't come down from the heavens to hook you up to an IV drip full of motivational fluids while you lay in bed and pray for change. You must wake up and help yourself. You have a God-given right to health, success, knowledge, justice, love, and joy, but nobody can manifest these in your life except yourself. We were all born with the tools to make things happen, and there is no room for pity parties, excuses, or blame games. Self-compassion does not mean allowing yourself to wilt and slump. You have a life purpose that wants to be carried out, but only self-love will give you the stamina to leave your legacy. To get a sense of satisfaction and contribute to the world around you, you must be fit in mind, body, and spirit. You can't offer your time, good advice, knowledge, talent, love, and support if you are sick, depressed, fatigued, numb, and confused. When you become an adult, your health and wellness become your sole responsibility, and there is nothing and no one else to blame for any prevalent hopelessness and destructiveness. It is in God's best interest that you practice love and kindness so that you can thrive in all areas of your life, but it starts with you and you only.

ON FOOD AND DIET

Your relationship with food can be indicative of your relationship with yourself. A great life is a life of balance, and the way you eat is not an exception. After years of exploring different diets and having just recently gotten certified as a holistic health coach, I can safely say that restriction does not work and that balance is key. No food is forbidden or intrinsically *good* or *bad* as long as it hasn't been highly processed or isn't artificial. There is a big lack of conscience with regard to dietary choices and our body's circadian rhythms that influence the way we digest food and how that impacts our overall well-being. Some slender, healthy, and toned people eat big, hearty meals, and we wonder how they get away with it. The composition of our physical bodies is a result of balance or a lack thereof and has nothing to do with eating a strictly low fat, low carb, paleo, vegan, or gluten-free diet. Restriction can be counterproductive in that deprivation feels like punishment, which leads to rebellion, which leads to binge eating, and people are bingeing on all the wrong foods. Highly refined, processed, and artificial foods are the real enemies. Not only do they leave us deprived of nutrients, but they also drastically spike insulin, making people insulin resistant. Your immune system depends on your gut health, and more and more people are developing metabolic syndrome as a direct result of dietary choices that are mismatched with our biochemistry. Our hormones are always trying to keep us alive and functioning, but if we saturate our bloodstream with excessive sugar and foreign ingredients, we give the body no option but to be on fight-or-flight mode all the time. So many people are struggling with a myriad of health issues and ignore that it all starts in the gut. Our food should be wholesome, nourishing, and served in balanced portions to keep our bodies vibrating high. It is important to educate yourself about the foods you eat and feed your family. Treating your body compassionately is crucial for it to function well and offer you a long life. What is a life of good service if you sail through it in a weak and diseased vessel?

On another note, if you are using food to fill your void, then it's best to treat your emotional turmoil first by getting rid of the false beliefs you hold about life, love, and yourself. Unlike drugs and alcohol, food won't go anywhere because you need it to survive, so it is easy to hide behind a food addiction. The good news is that becoming aware of your mistakes and setting new goals can help you reach balance in the way you eat so that you can use food to support you, not bloat you. Food is nourishment, and we have been bombarded with the phrase "You are what you eat," but it's important to consider that you are also how much you eat and what times you eat. The body seeks balance, which is why it is sophisticatedly designed to feel satiated when it's had enough food and to crave the nutrients it needs. There is a fine line between emotional cravings and physiological ones. Cravings that come from boredom, anxiety, depression, or grief are emotional cravings, and this is where food can become a crutch that aggravates us in the long run. To really care for the body, one must give it only what it needs and not oversaturate it with more food than it can handle. If your cravings are mainly stemming from a broken heart, you should know that you can help yourself by taking responsibility for your diet and making wiser choices. I have seen people recover from depression only by switching to a wholesome diet consisting mainly of vegetables, fruit, lean proteins, legumes, nuts, and seeds. Your physical body houses love, but it also absorbs all the density of the negative thoughts and feelings that block you, so how do you expect it to safely release all the built-up stress that it absorbs from your heart and soul if you feed it poorly? You can't ignore the body-mind-spirit connection when talking about diet because it is all intertwined. You can't expect your body to cooperate in healing your heart and soul if it is infested with toxins that it simultaneously has to clear up to function properly. Think of your whole being as a company that needs many hardworking employees to be successful. Of these employees, one-third of them are responsible for your mental department, another third are in charge of your emotional department, and the remaining third work on your physical department. You can't expect your company to be top notch if your mental- and emotional-department employees have to place their responsibilities on hold to assist the physical department that is being overworked all the time, can you? A balanced heart loves deeper when sitting in a balanced body, and a balanced body allows us to have more balanced thoughts. Treating your body kindly with nutrient-dense food and movement is vital for your overall wellness.

The way you metabolize your food is also influenced by the way you digest your life in general, so always have a way to channel out your stress. There are so many options to bring your heart and mind back to balance: journaling, exercising, meditating, or practicing mindful communication. Children have fast metabolisms not just because they have a young colon but because they have a young and innocent mind-set as well that allows them to digest and let go of stressful life situations with more ease than their older counterparts. There generally hasn't been enough time in a child's life to get plagued with enough fear and anxiety to block his or her digestion, so the child will eat whatever is on the menu and still enjoy fast elimination and nutrient absorption. This does not mean that we can safely feed our children all the fake foods on kids' menus. It is important to educate them on the way food choices directly impact the quality of our lives.

Emotional factors play a significant role in our dietary habits. We substitute love with food because the first sign of affection we received as newborns was through being fed. Mothers represent the concept of nourishment in our lives because they were the first ones to feed us when we were the most vulnerable and fragile. Infants who weren't offered a proper sense of nourishment and safety by their caregivers may drag those voids to adulthood and are more prone to struggle with eating disorders.

People who binge eat are not craving food as much as they are craving love, connection, and a sense of belonging. The problem is that food, like every other pleasure in life, will never be able to fulfill a person the way authentic love does. Luckily for you, taking a plunge into the past to try to figure out what went wrong isn't necessary. Life is an eternal present, so whatever happened before this moment is long gone and not worth going back to if it will take a toll on your emotions. The only thing that should matter is to become aware of your excessive hunger for love and embrace the idea that love starts with yourself. You must decide to stop using food to numb solitude and anxiety and make it your primary goal to focus on living your present moment without anticipation for the future or rancor for the past. A loving partner won't cure your anxiety, either, if you live a life trying to please everybody else's expectations and looking for that love and approval outside of yourself. Learning to forgive your past, letting go of resentment, and abstaining from judgment are great ways to start. Find the things you feel grateful for today, and keep focusing on being a compassionate and kind person. Get rid of your desire to be right amid conflicts with others, and choose to feel peace instead. Reach out to people in a loving way, and put your ego aside. The universe always responds to this with more love. Know that you are bountiful enough to offer yourself all the love and well-being that are your birthright, because you can. Love is available right now.

Your diet is meant to nourish and pleasure you, not punish and restrict you. If eating triggers feelings of anxiety, guilt, or shame, you are projecting onto your food an unresolved emotional wound that is in desperate need of healing. No struggle is in vain. Remember that healing happens when we return to love, and on the subject of compulsions, some things must go in order to reach this balance. You aren't afraid of fats and carbs; you are afraid of something deeper and using food to cope with this fear. Your beliefs form your thoughts, which form your actions, which form your habits, which ultimately form your reality, so you must get to the core of the problem. The habit is not the demon you can tackle. The real demon is the ingrained belief sitting in your subconscious mind that is perpetuating against your willpower. Soul-searching helps to bring into awareness the very fears, resistance, and guilt that are holding us back. Being conscious of yourself and your compulsions is the first thing to do on the path to wellness. Decide once and for all that your life starts now and that you don't have anything to feel anxious or guilty about or ashamed of. Those feelings do not serve you, and it's best to let them go. Paying attention to the cries of your soul is highly compassionate because nobody will decipher you better than yourself. You are the one who knows how you feel toward certain people, places, and situations, and if there is any speck of negativity in the mix, then you know you have some clearing to do. Your feelings define you in a way that you will never attract what you want but who you are. This is why diets don't work. You won't attract a perfect body and health by putting up a vision board full of bikini-body pictures and hitting the gym daily if your heart is plagued with hate, remorse, resentment, guilt, and shame. People who eat secretively, compulsively, or even starve themselves are people who are looking for a way out of their misery. They may feel overwhelmed, unloved, or invaded, and this is how they cope. In their case, food is not the principal enemy. The enemy is the poisonous set of false thoughts and affirmations that these people have adopted. At some point they chose to believe that they were unlovable, incomplete, compulsive, unstable, unworthy, reckless, deceitful, guilty, shameful, or addicted, and they never corrected that belief or did anything proactive about it. At some point they believed they were victims of another, so their hearts are heavy with resentment and hostility. Now they stuff their faces or fear food altogether, and they don't understand why. The mind is powerful, and eating disorders make sure to reflect back at us the very disordered thinking we adopted at different points of our lives or even the distorted perception of life we hold in the present moment. Food, like any other drug, is the thing we use to stuff this pain and anxiety down, so it is wise to tackle the pain first.

Anxiety aside, it is important to eat healthful foods, but it is also important to keep in mind that healthy eating is not about never touching a chocolate soufflé again or deeming carbs and fats as the devil. It is about balance, mindfulness, and nourishment. Not everyone took a crash course in nutrition, but it's not rocket science either. Eat clean, organic, fresh, and wholesome foods most of the time, and try to eat the least processed, refined, and artificial foods you can. There are no perfect diets! The best diet is the one that gets along with your digestion. You could thrive on being a carnivore, a vegetarian, a pescatarian, a fruitarian, or a vegan! I am not biased on diets because I respect that we all have different tastes and ideologies. My main goal is only to promote food for thought.

HEALING FROM ADDICTION

Every morning brings a new opportunity to start all over and to take responsibility for our thoughts and feelings one more time. What usually happens is that we wake up and go over all our responsibilities in our heads even before we set foot on the ground. From the moment we begin our routines, we go about our lives on autopilot and allow the same people, situations, or news headlines to trigger our anxiety, fears, judgment, and impatience. As the day progresses, we accumulate more and more stress with each negative reaction or thought we have because we continue to allow our emotions and brains to control us amid life's chaos. We forget that the frictions we come across are more a result of our mind-set and not tough luck, so we take offense, lose our patience, feel threatened, or get scared and throw ourselves out of balance. The disruption of our inner harmony is the mother of all discomfort and pain because housing negativity in our bodies lowers our energetic frequency. Vibrating low is the main reason our immune systems weaken, so we get physical disease and discomfort such as headaches, bloating, constipation, cravings, and other more severe symptoms. We forget that it all began with our own feeling and thought patterns, so we blame others and allow external factors to control our well-being. This is how we accumulate karma because karma is nothing more than the buildup of detrimental beliefs and reactions that detonate a negative charge all over our energetic field, which in turn goes on attracting more energy of its kind. Frustration arises when we find ourselves in a vicious circle of reacting negatively and attracting negative things because we attract all the things that perfectly resonate with the quality of our thoughts and emotions. This is why I believe harmony is our biggest asset. Our balance is our most prized possession. You protect your material assets with a shield and a sword, so why wouldn't you do the same with your good energy, which is the real source of your wealth? Why do you allow people and external factors to rob you of your most valuable gift? You are powerful enough to keep your balance in check and decide to feel good most of the time.

Your power is in your center, where the waters have a steady, calm, and serene flow. Straying away from your center to the polarities, where the waters are either dead or too choppy, is not a happy place for you. Our center is in our heart. This is where we get charged with positivity and light, so when we misalign from our core, we lose some of that precious light and immediately feel a void. Our voids are nothing more than empty spaces that were left dark and are looking to be lit again. Stress, blame, anxiety, fear, anger, and hate open up huge voids in our souls, and this is why we feel *empty inside.* The stressed-out person then goes out and binges on food, pops pills, gets drunk, takes drugs, has shallow sex, gambles savings away, and stretches his or her voids even wider. Addictive substances and behaviors give us a temporary high as they trigger the release of endorphins and dopamine into our bloodstream, but this bliss is short-lived because shedding light on the symptoms is *not* the equivalent of shedding light on the cause. Taking a pill or drinking a cocktail that numbs out your feelings of despair does not brighten up the negative thought patterns that brought about your voids in the first place. The external things we use to get away from our negative feelings give us a temporary bliss. Only the bliss that we tap into and access from within is permanent. All the side effects of addictive substances are there to remind us of how they are not the ultimate cure or the answer to our prayers because as soon as the physical effect of the drug subsides, we find ourselves right back where we started. You wake up the next morning after a night of excessive indulgence and realize that not only is the bundle of negativity that you tried to numb out still stuck within you, but now you have more issues to deal with after you went out on a limb the night before and got yourself into trouble. This is how karma is formed. Do you now realize why allowing others to dishearten you is the most irresponsible thing you can do? No one is out to hurt you. You have the power to guard your inner peace and make sure that nothing and no one steals it from you because really, nobody can. Only you can dim your own light by the power of your perception. If you perceive threat, hate, obstacles, and misfortune, that is exactly what you will get more of.

Addiction is so prevalent because it is the easy exit, and people love shortcuts. Nobody wants to put in the real work. Instant gratification is what desperate souls look for when they can't figure themselves out, and the industries that benefit from that weakness will always make sure to keep selling tempting outlets or temporary fixes. Nobody will fix you but yourself. You are responsible to walk a straight line and not let anyone else throw you off balance. When it comes to addictions and compulsions, it is important to realize that there is a false set of beliefs stuck somewhere in your subconscious that is making you react to life in all the wrong ways. If you don't tap into these blocking perceptions to straighten them out, they will keep steering the wheel of your vehicle toward people and experiences that represent them best. This is what the universe does: it pairs you up to the reality that matches your most ingrained beliefs. You are no victim of destiny or a weak, unlucky soul. You have the most powerful tool to heal, called intention, and you can intend right now to become the best version of yourself and live the life of your dreams. Your dreams are not there in vain; they are visible to you in the depth and breadth of your imagination so that you can get a picture of what's possible for you. All you desire is already happening in a parallel universe; you just have to access it through your faith. Being healed of addiction is one of those parallel realities, and faith alone will walk you through the steps you must take to adopt the consciousness of that healed person you are ready to become. Never give up; it does not happen overnight, but there is no rush because time makes you stronger, wiser, and younger, not the opposite.

Healing from any type of addiction or compulsion requires you to embrace your unaltered state of consciousness because it is through your human awareness that you can shift your perception to transform you. You can't awaken to the truth if a part of your soul is dwelling in nothingness. Nothingness is where numbing food, drugs, narcotics, and alcohol take you. It is that place where you are not awake and not dreaming either. You are unconscious and ignorant. Ignorance is the state of not knowing where one lacks awareness in general, so it is accurate to say that ignorance is the equivalent of being asleep and powerless. There is not much to do or feel bad about in a state of ignorance, but no glory or joy will sprout from it either. Addiction, therefore, keeps you dormant and robs your life of the passion and joy that can only manifest through the awakening of your self-awareness. Being self-aware means that you understand how your physical and spiritual bodies support each other for a greater good. Self-realization happens when you realize who you really are and the potential you are made of. We have a higher self that connects us to all humanity, as it is the source of all existence, but we also have a human self that is unique and has its own particular talents and desires. When you embrace the totality of who you are in body, mind, and spirit, you start to live. Self-realization is not the finish line but the starting point. The moment you realize that the world around you is essentially a reflection of who you are as a whole, you will activate your unique potential, break free from the perception of separateness, and begin to heal. Your senses are meant to walk you through this process of self-realization, so in a way your senses are God's biggest gift to you! They are the ones that help you experience life as it is, process your emotions, connect to your higher source to tap into all universal wisdom, and grow stronger.

How are you meant to identify with others, get a feel of the world around you, and process all the physical stimuli that want to propel you to great heights if you've made it a habit to numb your senses? A big chunk of the population is hooked on alcohol, cigarettes, anxiety pills, painkillers, and other desensitizing drugs. Food can also be addictive when used as a numbing agent. MRI studies have shown that sugar consumption lights up the very same part of the brain that lights up when dosing cocaine and heroin. On the subject of liquor, most of society looks forward to happy hours and associates alcohol consumption with good times. For centuries, societies have celebrated good news, dealt with rough patches, and helped themselves be more extroverted by using recreational drugs, so to say that they are self-destructive may be frowned upon by many. These crutches can sabotage self-love. I have seen many people make unfavorable and destructive life choices while under the influence of drugs, alcohol, narcotics, and the like. They all weaken the body and, even if to a small degree, take over us and distort our thoughts, words, and actions and rob us of our authentic selves. Authenticity makes us sharp, real, kosher, reliable, trustworthy, and faithful. Getting high makes us prone to say things, do things, and even think thoughts that aren't aligned with our truth. This makes us take three steps back in our progress, and it tarnishes our dignity. If you are prohibited to drive a motor vehicle while under the influence of a drug, what makes you able to drive your body vehicle around? If you aren't suited to handle a car, you aren't suited to handle yourself, let alone others. Period. It is a hard pill to swallow, I know. It took me three years to fully recover from my social crutch of dependence, but I can tell you, the rewards are huge.

When we go through life trying to figure ourselves out, forgive others, and learn to get along without judgment, resorting to food and drugs is common when the hard feelings take over and dim our light. It is so easy to rest from the density of our negative feeling overload by indulging in things that instantly stimulate our brains to release dopamine and endorphins. Our hearts know right from wrong and will always lead us back to love, but when our ego takes over and clouds our judgment with self-destructive thoughts, the confusion can soar to high levels of angst and despair, which is where addiction and compulsions come into play. Inner turmoil can be set off by something as grave as sexual harassment or by getting rejected by your peers. Anything that causes someone to feel shame, guilt, inadequacy, or unworthiness or promotes secrecy can lead a person to resort to numbing agents to bear the heavy burden. Knowing how to wisely handle negative thoughts and emotions should be a class offered in grade school, as it is the main problem faced by society, from my own humble perspective. Our minds are not properly trained from an early age to ward off negativity and honor love, no matter the circumstance.

Many grow up not knowing how to proactively channel their trapped emotions or how to speak their minds without judgment, and they become resentful and defensive adults. Being able to see yourself in another and practice compassion, tolerance, and goodwill, knowing that we are set up to live a great life if we only trust our guiding light, is the mind-set of fulfillment. Unfortunately, those who disconnect from this truth end up feeling so lost and hopeless that they become compulsive people looking for relief in all the wrong places.

I have dealt with addictive-compulsive disorders and used to think that I could save myself by keeping my inner turmoil a secret and thinking happy thoughts, but to think one can heal without external support is part of the problem. Of course, ultimate healing is achieved by one's own shift in perception, but allowing others to guide you through the process is imperative because many times the root of the problem is dug deep in our subconscious mind. Past trauma and shocking experiences are blocked out by our minds as a survival mechanism to protect the heart from the pain they caused. The problem is that the distorted beliefs that were adopted from such trauma were sent to the back seat of the car and are bossing the driver around without us even realizing it. This is how our subconscious minds work. Unless we grab a mop and broom and break into that dark room controlling our lives to clean up the mess that is leading us to self-sabotage, we will never move forward. Our consciousness alone won't cooperate much because even it doesn't understand where its impulses come from, as it has been acting on autopilot for years and years. To have a support system aid us in dissolving our fears and resentment makes a huge difference, as their perspective of our pain can help bring light to the issues we have not been wanting to acknowledge on our own. You do have everything you need to heal, but sometimes those healing tools are locked up in a safe that you lost the keys to, and the help of others can help you break that safe open. Keep in mind that isolation is good for introspection and meditation but not for evolution. We need others on our path of self-fulfillment. We aren't capable of evolving on our own, even as adults! We need moral and loving support from our peers, just like we need the earthly elements to stay alive. Part of allowing others to help you on your journey is giving yourself permission to trust the people around you. Those who become defensive from past trauma stopped trusting others at some point in their lives and feel the safest in emotional isolation. They can put themselves out there physically, but their emotions are locked down, and they won't allow themselves to be vulnerable. An isolated heart yearns to give and receive love, so when the person doesn't allow that love to pour in from relying on other people, the vicious circle of addiction and compulsion will continue.

The person trying to get better must know that healing does not happen overnight. Patience is a much-needed virtue on the path to recovery because tapping into your subconscious programs is layers deep. The good news is you don't have to dread the journey because huge satisfaction comes every time you take a step up the ladder. Self-discovery can be very gratifying and eye opening in spite of the stumbles or the darkness one might find. When you come face-to-face with the dark demons of your past, you realize that the love you are made of is much stronger and there was never anything or anyone mightier than the light torch you carry. It takes courage and determination, but you are never alone. Setting the intention to heal will attract to you all the necessary components to help you take the blindfold off and live in love and clarity. I personally recommend meditation and pranayama (breathing) exercises, as they allow us to tap into our souls by being mindful of our bodies through stillness and focus. Setting an intention to heal your pain and asking the body to release it in every exhale can be very transforming. In the midst of the calmness that meditation provides, you can scan your body for any somatic tension or discomfort accumulated from past trauma and start forgiving the images that pop up in your head as you breathe light into every memory.

It is so unfortunate to get hooked on desensitizing drugs because the senses are our intuitive life compasses. If we don't mindfully decode the signals our body is picking up, we are prone to make unwise decisions, as there is no wisdom without intuition. When you get high or drunk, the subtle wire that connects your body to your spirit gets tangled up, and you get lost. It might give you a sense of *letting go*, but the only thing you are letting go of is your emotional and mental intelligence, nothing else.

Your ego will tell you you're in for a ride and that you deserve that mind-altering fix while your spirit suffers. Drugs and alcohol are like emergency exit doors. They offer a seductive chance to eject yourself from the present moment, and when you do, you get lost. There is nothing promising, joyful, or satisfying outside the present moment. Our power lies in our awareness and in our presence. When we get high or drunk, we shut down our instincts and sabotage our life purpose, because great ideas that want to enter the mind through our intuition are immediately sent back to where they came from. Ideas come to us at unpredictable times, so if you numb yourself at decisive moments, you will lose the divine guidance that was ready to take you where you needed to go. Being high can give you a false sense of calmness and courage, but it is actually making you more anxious and fearful because when you come out of the trance, you realize everything is the same. Not only did the drug trip solve nothing, but you come out of its daze with a lower frequency that robs you of your natural problem-solving skills and healing capacity. Addiction is a cruel disease.

Your soul is nothing more than a body of light energy with transformative power. It can take your negativity and make it positive. It can take you from lack to abundance and heal your pain, and it does all this through mindfulness. Fear is the perpetrator of all disease. It is quite fascinating to understand how fear works. First, *fate* presents you with a person, place, or thing that scares the life out of you. Second, you believe this person, place, or thing to be real and feel threatened. Third, you feel sorry for yourself and believe you are a victim. Fourth, the fear, defensiveness, self-pity, and low self-esteem slightly separate your body from your spirit. Fifth, this separation opens a dark and lonely void in your entire being. Sixth, this void makes you agitated, anxious, and depressive, so you look for numbing medicine. Seventh, you find food, sex, gambling, drugs, and alcohol. That's it. You forget that the way to tap back into your healing spirit is by consciously reprogramming the initial fear that set you up for self-sabotage. Instead of staying awake and working on their subconscious programs, people find it easier to give their emotions a sleeping pill, but our issues get resolved by mindfully working on our thoughts and feelings within our physical bodies, not outside of them.

Remember that you are essentially made of pure energy, not a body. You have the power to heal your body and emotions through mindful awareness and an open heart. Your allopathic and recreational drugs are just treating the physical symptoms, not the cause of your ailments. This is why so many people have recurring health issues. Ultimately, every issue you have is an energetic one without exception. The solution to everything is energetic. If you don't change your energetic field by shifting your negative perception of life into a positive one, you won't be able to heal your physical body. Plain and simple.

On the subject of sobriety, I just want to comment that recreational drugs work as social lubricants, but they beat our true purpose, because we are naturally social beings. We were born to relate, so if we approach new people in a slightly stupefied state, we sabotage our human nature. Why do we need a social lubricant? To numb anxiety? What are we anxious about? A new experience? Are we intimidated by new interactions? Why do they feel threatening? I always want to explore my anxiety, not numb it. Anxiety comes to us fueled with purpose. It wants us to face a part of ourselves that wants to bloom but is too scared to do so. When we numb ourselves with depressants, we might approach others with more flow and ease, but this approach is not authentic. Connecting with others is best done awake, even if it feels intimidating at first. It's supposed to be intimidating! Our souls are wise, and they know about perfect timing when it comes to opening up to others. Our instinct reads new people and tells us when it's safe to proceed or hold back. We should not force ourselves with social lubricants to bring out a personality that is not ready to come out naturally. It is perfectly normal to feel shy and reserved when mingling with strangers. The right people will pick up on your genuine energy and will approach you in a genuine way. Who has time for fake encounters?

Relating to new people becomes more interesting and gratifying when done so with a conscious mind, as it shows self-respect and self-love. If you treat yourself with love, respect, and compassion, what do you think is bound to happen? Others will naturally feel compelled to treat you the same way too. It's the infallible law of attraction. You attract what you are because you are what you feel. If you feel stupefied, you'll attract folly. Yes, it can be intimidating to meet new people in your full senses if you aren't used to it. When you go out, it can help to think that you will bump into God's different faces because God is everywhere! You don't need to feel intimidated by he who is in all the new people you meet too. Folks who are out and about without the need for drugs and liquor are confident enough to be themselves. You can explore sobriety more and see where it takes you. Just remember that you are always free to choose how you treat yourself, but you are not immune to the consequence of your choice.

I love thinking that you are capable of accessing your fullest potential on this very moment because self-realization happens when you understand that loving, accepting, and forgiving emancipate you from the chains of misery. Compulsive behavior is nothing more than your soul's cry for balance. It desperately wants you to embrace the duality that you are made of instead of stuffing or drowning it down with numbing substances. You don't just wake up and decide to recover from bad habits unless you are ready to make significant changes in the way you translate the world around you. Recovery won't happen overnight. Getting rid of your inner demons is a task that is constantly worked on through trial and error. Having a slip up does not mean that you don't have it in you to heal. Stumbling on the path to wellness is just a sign that you are putting in the effort, and that intention alone will pay off. This I promise you. Never give up. It is of utmost importance to stay present. Never look back on your transformative journey, and don't force instant results, either, because there is a perfect timing for everything, even for milestones. Many elements come to play when it comes to getting better. It is not just about staying sober, eating less, forgiving your past, or facing certain fears. When we awaken after years of living on autopilot, we encounter many surprises that we weren't ready for and new lessons or discoveries that we weren't anticipating. Every factor that surges is there to aid us, but we can become frustrated in wanting to get out of our own way too fast instead of allowing life to take its course naturally. Life isn't trying to bombard you with a myriad of testing situations. You are simply meant to encounter all shades of life's spectrum and practice a balanced mind-set and balanced attitude so that riding the waves of your life can become a hobby instead of a burden.

Accomplishments are seldom due to willpower—this I guarantee you. None of us is weak at will; we are just not present. People struggling with addictions and compulsions have their hearts stuck in the past and their eyes set on the future. You won't extinguish your body's compulsions through sheer resoluteness or strength of character because character is a product of nobility, not the cause. Staying away from gluten, dairy, caffeine, sugar, and processed foods won't heal you from obesity, bulimia, anorexia, or binge eating. Staying away from liquor won't heal you from alcoholism, and staying away from drugs won't make your cravings for them go away. Bingeing is nothing more than the symptom of a spiritual imbalance and has nothing to do with your physical body, so you might as well stop trying to control your body and focus on controlling your heart and mind instead. Your spirit wants *balance*. There is a little confusion on the meaning of balance, by the way. People think there is no balance in sobriety, for instance. They believe that not drinking any alcohol and taking any drugs whatsoever are extreme choices, not balanced ones. They convince themselves that they need a fix of something because we are all meant to "live a little," but balance isn't reached by numbing ourselves. Balance is only accomplished in a state of full awareness. Being fully aware means your spirit is present and anchored in this moment. Bingeing on addictive substances yanks us away from the now.

Compulsions are your soul's intent to leave this moment because you are subconsciously trying to evade something in your presence. Being present shows you all that is in front of you that you might have been trying to avoid for years. It could be a thought, a feeling, or an intuition. It could be a person or a place that triggers unresolved issues from the past or fears of the future. Whichever the case, ejecting yourself from the now by indulging in different distractions gives you a false sense of joy. May your compulsions teach you a valuable lesson: there is no real joy found anywhere other than right now. Addicted people are always anticipating their next fix to get relief. They just move from one compulsion to another because they aren't centered. They still feel lost and disconnected as they sail through life's ups and downs. We can be physically sober, but what good is sobriety if we are spiritually unprepared to cope with our emotions? We need to learn how to handle our angst and fears first. Taking away the food and the drugs is not the solution. We get hooked not because we are weak but because we are detached. Beating ourselves up for failed attempts when wanting to heal is a waste of time and energy because failing has nothing to do with our character or integrity. Failing is a result of being out of touch with reality. Reality is what we have now, not what we had yesterday or what we expect to have tomorrow. Addiction stems from the anxiety we get when resenting the past and anticipating the future. Balance is found now.

I have heard people say (and I used to believe this myself) that addiction is hereditary and that those suffering from addiction are victims of fate. The only thing we are a victim of is of being taught how to cope with life in destructive ways when we imitated the way our grandparents and parents dealt with life. Behavioral patterns are the real hereditary obstacles we must overcome. Compulsions are the consequence of a person who grew up with much fear. People who were taught to face life in defensive and hostile ways have no idea what it means to surrender and love unconditionally. There's still a side of them that believes in the concept of tomorrow, so all their bets are placed on the future. There's always been a side of them that does not believe in being happy right now because they could always have a more loving partner, a bigger bank account, further travels, a healthier body, more friendships, a tighter family, a nicer home (or more homes for that matter), a pricier car, stronger muscles, or a more lucrative job. They become obsessed, and they try to control it all. They must control the outcome of things so they can get all they desire because right now they're not good enough. They can always be more and have more. Obsessive compulsions are very common with overachievers. Overachievers start by thinking that when they are thinner, stronger, wealthier, prettier, famous, funnier, or popular, they'll be able to get engaged, find the man or woman of their dreams, travel more, become a parent, walk out of a choking relationship, be free, inspire, be happy, be worthy, or find peace. They don't believe that all this can happen now because it's always anticipated to happen in the near future. They can't fathom how self-realization is pure presence. They think that achievement happens only after certain steps are taken, and even when a goal is reached, their joy is short-lived. Overachievers live in a constant pursuit of love and fulfillment outside of themselves.

If you are going to adopt a new habit, let it be the habit of anchoring yourself to this moment. Observe the world around you. Learn to pay attention to the way people are without wanting to change anything. Learn to look for the clues and signs God is sending you all the time through the sights and scenes in your realm of perception. Learn to breathe in the midst of tension and identify with all the good and the bad around you. Life is a manifestation of your consciousness, so pay attention to what you are conscious of, and learn to perceive things through a lens of love and compassion. Learn to forgive and to abstain from judgment. We are all one and the same. Focus on today, and let go of your past; let go of your future. They don't exist. Learn to think of today as a never-ending now and let go of expectations. Learn to access the love within you and stop looking for it in the approval of others. Learn to love your body and guard your thoughts the same way you guard your prized possessions. Learn to find yourself in the eyes of another because that is where a part of you already exists. The only reason you binge is because of the void you have dug within by detaching yourself from the now and expecting things to happen tomorrow. This void is so deep that nothing fills it up. Why do you think AA meetings preach the phrase "one day at a time"? They ask alcoholics to focus on this day only because there is really no tomorrow. Tomorrow and the next moment exist only in our heads. Embrace the idea that there's nothing to heal from in the present. People think of healing in the future because they can't conceive that now has all the answers and relief. Your addictions are just trying to pull you back to the present moment where your full potential and endless love reside.

Use people to gauge your level of presence. If you avoid certain people or get uncomfortable with the remarks or actions of others, you will have found great opportunities to anchor yourself back to the present. Many times we want to run away or ignore people or things that happen around us to avoid feeling vulnerable, but to embrace that which we resist is one of the most compassionate things we can do for ourselves. Relating to other people offers us the chance to look at ourselves because whatever we see in others is a reflection of a repressed side of ours. Whatever we haven't forgiven or accepted in us will call for our attention through the presence of another. You are made of all the good and all the bad that you come into contact with. Human beings can't evolve without relationships because it is through them that we get to make amends with the universe and with ourselves. We weren't gifted with a consciousness and ability to rationalize so that we could do it in isolation. We make sense of things and evolve through human interaction. Even the man who is stranded on a deserted island finds the strength to survive because he is motivated to get back to his tribe or family. People who avoid human contact are in a way trying to avoid themselves because people work like mirrors, and if they aren't ready to see themselves in the eyes of another, they will surely prefer to spend more time alone. It is when we have to relate and look at others in the eye that we get the most anxious and want to drink, smoke, or eat. Food and drugs help to tame this anxiety. We fear that if we open up our hearts to whatever is happening in front of us, we will find gnarly things like emptiness, rejection, disapproval, threat, abandonment, betrayal, humiliation, loneliness, failure, or incompleteness, so we'd rather put up a wall instead.

Sometimes we feel like eating an entire tray of pastries not because we are physically starving but because we are spiritually starved, afraid, and looking for comfort. Unfortunately, we often find a reason to feel afraid: "Did my partner not cuddle me enough tonight because I'm not lovable anymore? Did I make a fool of myself earlier today when I spoke to that crowd? Did I look terrible in my outfit at that event this morning? Did I not get a callback because I was terrible in my interview? Is my spouse cheating on me? Will they refuse to renew my sponsorship? Are my parents mad at me for not visiting them this weekend? Have my children become distant because I was too harsh with them? Will I get fat because I skipped the gym this afternoon? Will I be able to travel to my sibling's wedding? Are they gossiping about me behind my back? Am I going to get fired at the most unexpected moment? Am I in the right place at the right time? Am I wasting my life away? Will I ever get married? Why can't I conceive? Oh my gosh, we have turbulence! Is this plane going to crash?" We accumulate fears and take ourselves to our own emotional limits where we hit a wall and then look for a cure that is many times sought in food, booze, sex, slot machines, and pills, which provide a temporary joyride. After the high subsides, people come back to face the very same fears feeling bloated, hung over, or fatigued. Double whammy.

All the fears you have concerning your relationships or the outcome of your life have been fabricated in your head. The impulses you get to eat, drink, or medicate are so intense because that's how bad you want to numb your negative assumptions. You have divinely attracted all the things that bother and threaten you so that you can face them once and for all because unless you do, you'll keep suffering the consequences of your own mental tricks. Everything you perceive in the world is serving your purpose. Pay close attention when another person's behavior triggers your insecurities because everything that scares you, offends you, or hurts you is just trying to heal you. You are made of spirit, and no one can threaten spirit. If another person makes you mad or sad, think of him or her whom angels sent down from heaven to help you rise and overcome. Don't react defensively, but wish them the best. Pray that they do well in life because if they do well, you do well. What happens to others is happening to you because the world is nothing but a reflection of your perception. If all you do is wish others well, you will flood yourself with so much good energy that amazing things will inevitably happen to you too. All that makes us feel like we are bound to crash and burn is just trying to teach us to surrender. It is OK to be afraid but not to stay afraid. It is fine to stumble but not to stay on the ground. Life comes with dark patches, but they are there to strengthen us, not keep us in the dark. The purpose of darkness is to help us bounce back to light, so in a way darkness can be exciting if you learn how to work with it. To get lit up in the dark means to give in to whatever the moment holds without judgment, resentment, or tension. We are all made of vibrant light meant to brighten up the dark, not the other way around. Darkness can't extinguish a flame.

You are everything that ever was, is, and will be. You're made of love, hate, health, disease, wisdom, and ignorance. If you weren't capable of hating, you'd have no idea what loving feels like. You represent every possibility in the universe. The reason you think you are addicted today and can heal tomorrow is because you are already both. There is no time and space except in our heads, so every possibility is already happening in a parallel universe. We live in an infinite present where everything already exists. You get to experience what you focus on. If you avoid living in this moment, you will cheat yourself from experiencing the life you desire. If you constantly feel like there must be more to life than what you are going through, then you are probably right, but move in the direction of your dreams and aspirations in a state of gratefulness for what already is.

If you have goals and dreams that fuel your motivation, then keep dreaming and working proactively toward them! The only thing that sabotages our desires is avoiding the negativity that the present may bring. You can't expect life to always be the way you want it, and it's best to be prepared to encounter whatever life brings. Dark patches should not be mightier than your light and wisdom. A friend once advised me to not be afraid of the dark, but I never really understood what he meant. I thought he was encouraging me to indulge in my self-destructive habits without fear of the consequences. I thought his suggestion was tempting and irresponsible. Now that I look back, I fully understand the wisdom behind his remark. To embrace the dark does not mean to cut one's veins, hurt somebody, down a bottle of tequila, or binge and purge chocolate cake. To befriend the dark means to surrender to your anxiety, fear, and sadness instead of numbing them. To welcome and breathe into your anguish and pain is the most powerful way to heal. When something hurts, we are used to reacting instead of acting. We curse, self-medicate, binge, complain, demand, restrict, avoid, whine, escape, and punish. This is everything that embracing the dark *does not* mean. Negativity is here to make us better people, not to turn us into escapists. Facing your dark side means accepting your negativity as part of your wholesome makeup. Fear and sadness are as natural and necessary as love and joy. Self-sabotage occurs when we punish ourselves for feeling down as if feeling down were sinful or weak. Guess what? We are sinners, and we are weak. We are human beings made of physical flesh and a nonphysical spirit. We are made of weak and strong, light and dark, black and white, yin and yang! Open your doors to the dark when it pays you a visit, and let it sit next to you. Your fear is just reflecting back at you the duality that you are made of, and you should compassionately breathe into it, not ever escape it. If something scares you, I suggest you focus on that fear and tell it, "Yes, you exist, but only in my imagination, and you don't serve me right now, so I will kindly let you go. I know only the best will happen." Your fear only wants to be acknowledged before it goes back to where it came from. Fear has to exist so that we understand love. If you shut down fear, it will keep coming back to haunt you until you give it the time of day. Don't be afraid to face the dark.

Failing at something doesn't make you a failure. Failure also has to exist so that we understand triumph. All setbacks and stumbles are redirecting us in the right way. We must respect the concept of perfect timing and have faith that the universe always has the best outcome in store for us. Stay positive and bounce back to light because you are both positive and negative. You have it in you to achieve to the degree that you failed. There is perfection and divinity in everything that happens to you right now, and this includes your compulsions. Learning to see the bright side of darkness is imperative for you to manifest great things. Identifying with your flaws instead of trying to run away from them is part of the equation. Embrace the idea that you are addiction, compulsion, and failure to the same degree that you are health, balance, and success. You decide which emotional outfit you want to wear today.

EXERCISE TO ACTIVATE

The body needs movement. Movement helps us activate our bodies because when we move, blood starts to flow, oxygen gets carried to each and every one of our cells, and we rejuvenate from within. Don't tell yourself that you can do without exercise because you're fine with your weight. Exercise is not just about weight management. It is about pumping life into your system! Something magical happens when you engage in physical activity because you suddenly become aware of your body, you start to pay attention to the present moment, and you enter a sort of meditative state. It's not just about shedding and toning but also about enlivening and activating. When I go out for a jog or a hike, I come back home with new ideas. What happens is that the blood flow activated through movement reaches our brain and highly stimulates creativity. If you ever feel stuck and need to get your creative juices flowing, exercising can be a very helpful and kind act for yourself because it also raises your vibration. When your vibration is high, not only do you feel better, but it also allows you to manifest more goodness and to become a hands-on creator of your destiny. A high vibration also strengthens your immune system and can protect you against illness and disease.

Exercise is also amazing for channeling out stress and accumulated tension. Yoga workouts are the best for this kind of therapy. Through flexibility and breathing poses, yoga allows you to activate your energy centers and to become aware of your body. Some people cry in the middle of a yoga practice as stuck energy gets released through movement, breath, and awareness in the form of sweat and tears. All exercise can be truly cathartic in this sense.

BABY STEPS

All self-compassionate acts come with some resistance because it's much easier to take shortcuts. It requires less effort to escape, avoid, and focus on the external world instead of inwardly, where all our answers are. We must start being compassionate with ourselves if we are to love and care for others. A person who self-destructs has very little good energy left to nurture others, build strong relationships, or take their lives to skyrocketing levels. The good thing is that you don't have to overwhelm yourself trying to adopt clean-cut habits overnight. Baby steps are naturally effective when wanting to make a change. Little babies don't learn to sprint and swim overnight, so why should we? Take it one step at a time, and don't beat yourself up if you stumble. Once you start incorporating new habits that make you feel good about yourself, you'll be better able to focus on all the people you interact with. You will have more love to give, more experiences to share, and more to look forward to.

It works wonders to start slow with anything in life, especially when trying new things that feel so foreign to us. Starting slow is a great way to adopt a new habit. Don't try to jog three miles on the first day of your fitness challenge! Start slow, jog half a mile, and work yourself up at your own pace. This is a great way to respect your process and build more self-compassion. Don't try to eat all healthy foods overnight if you've never followed a healthy diet. Start by eliminating one processed food at a time so as to not overwhelm yourself. It is when we strive for perfection from the start that we are bound to fail. Don't try to hike the whole mountain trail in a flash if you're not conditioned yet! You will likely exhaust yourself and lose motivation to do it again. Take your time, start slow, and listen to your body. The same goes for everything else in life. Take compassionate baby steps.

KINDNESS AND TOLERANCE

The universe is so impeccably synchronized that every single person who is in your life, the city you currently live in, the job you work in or the unemployment you now experience, your finances, and the dilemmas you find yourself in are absolutely perfect. Everything that happens to us and everyone whom we interact with are there to show us more patience, compassion, tolerance, empathy, sympathy, and love. All the things you *think* you didn't choose to experience, like a lack of funds, a miscarriage, a divorce, being laid off from work, not finding a job, being single, being married, getting deported, failing a test, catching a cold, losing a loved one, getting stuck in traffic, missing a flight, or even misplacing your car keys and being late to a meeting, are all blessings in disguise meant to bring you back to balance. It can be hard to digest this idea, but it's true. Many people survived the 9/11 terrorist attacks because they were stuck in traffic that day. They probably didn't know this on a conscious level, but their souls did because spirit knows it all. Their spirits weren't ready to leave this physical realm just yet, so synchronicity made sure to delay them that morning. Why am I saying this? To develop more gratitude and tolerance for the things that don't always go the way we want them to and to be kinder to ourselves and to others amid circumstances that are truly just there just to teach us something golden.

You have the capacity to be compassionate with everyone, all the time. You have enough benevolence in your heart to love anybody, regardless of who he or she is or what that person represents in your life. Do you really think you are just compatible with some and clash with others? As mentioned before, compatibility and compassion stem from the late Latin word *compati,* which means "to suffer with." It's not that you will suffer with others to form a bond with them, no. When you are compatible with a person, it is because you have learned to feel compassion for him or her. You have shared so much together that you have had the opportunity to connect with the other soul in the good times and the bad. You have tapped into his or her vulnerable side in a way that you now see beyond flaws and find it easier to forgive wrongdoings. You have developed compassion for the person; you are now compatible. Every single person who is walking around in our physical reality or realm of perception deserves our love, compassion, and respect, and this includes coworkers, bosses, distant relatives, friends of friends, and even the cashier at the grocery store. Why? Because we placed them there, believe it or not. They are serving us in ways we can't even imagine. They are the teachers we called for in this lifetime to show us the things we need to see, to speak out loud the things we need to hear, and to act out the things that move us in order to learn our much-needed lessons and become our best selves.

When we are about to blame someone for the way we feel, for the way we live, or for the way we think, learn to press the pause button and take responsibility for your own life. Nobody is responsible for your reality but you. The people who don't take responsibility for their own misery are the ones who suffer the most. Those who refuse to own their emotions are driven by their egos. They find it easy to just throw the towel and give up on people because they'd rather be proudly right than humbly responsible, and they jump from one relationship to another, repeating the same patterns. Their next relationship might not be the exact same replica of their last failed one, but it will evoke the same feelings of frustration, loneliness, uncertainty, betrayal, separateness, instability, uncertainty, fear, anxiety, boredom, abuse, abandonment, and ultimate failure, unless the lesson in love is learned. I'm not saying to stay in painful relationships, but I am suggesting giving up arguments, taking responsibility for your reactions, leaving amicably, and feeling grateful for the learning experience it offered. It is much more gratifying to develop the compassionate power within you to forgive. If you must take a different route, you must at least move on in peace after having deciphered the lesson that given relationship brought to support your spiritual growth. You must be able to look that person in the eye and feel nothing but appreciation, respect, and compassion. If there is still an ounce of resentment, anger, remorse, hate, bitterness, or any other hard feeling toward the person you have distanced yourself from, then the lesson has not been learned. You can rest assured someone else is on the way to help you soften that heart of yours by pushing your buttons again until you pluck out those negative feelings from your heart. Life does not have to be that complicated. You really have the power to surrender and heal *right now* by being compassionate. Don't wait.

We are all nothing but mirrors of each other. The person you deem abominable is always reflecting back that part of them that you are also capable of becoming. We are capable of being just as violent, aggressive, selfish, narcissistic, evil, corrupt, and destructive as those we point the finger at. As human beings, we are made of right and wrong, flaws and perfection, and not only light but also darkness. Why do you think we have free will? As human beings, it is our biggest responsibility to make use of our free will to do good. We were given the power to love just as we were given the power to hate. We were given the power to succeed just as we were given the power to fail. It really is all up to us. This is how powerful we are. Everything that happens to us is a product of our free will. We have the choice to blame and victimize just as we have the choice to empower ourselves and overcome. It is only one decision away, and this one choice is available to us twenty-four seven. You can't judge others, because you have the power to mess up just as severely as them, and this is why their mistakes and wrongdoings strongly tempt you to pass judgment.

We all have a background. We were all born innocent and pure. We were all molded. We were all programmed with different belief systems. We all observed and got our examples from different role models. Some were born lacking; others were born opulent. It can therefore be safe to conclude that we all operate differently because of our different mental chips and accumulated neurosis, but one thing is for sure: *we are all on the quest for love*. We all want to go back to our unblemished origins. From the moment we were born, life's trials clouded our purity and loving nature. We got confused when we came face-to-face with the duality of life on earth, and some lost more faith than others. Some retracted into fear more than others. In spite of our different backgrounds and upbringings, we all strive for the same: to love and be loved. Compassion comes easy when we understand this.

Believe that nobody is out to harm you. Believe that nobody can rob you of your belongings or of your loved ones. Believe that nobody can abuse you. Believe that nobody can imprison you or pluck your wings. Nobody except you has the power to bring you down. When you sense that someone poses a threat, read the signs and move in a different direction if need be, but don't resent the person thinking he or she has power over you. The only way another person becomes more powerful than you is when you believe he or she is more powerful. Your belief deposits that much energy in his or her hands, and you become vulnerable to his or her negativity. If someone is acting negatively toward you, remember the truth of the matter: "All is well because all they want is love. I asked for this to further develop my tolerance and kindness. They are my reflection. By loving them I am loving myself. God will take care of the rest."

You better believe God will take care of the rest. The universe will make things right. All that is up to you is to keep an open heart and to see the good in people, and you'll be surprised at how things start to fall into place. You might ask, "But I was just robbed! You suggest I just relax and think that the robber is needy of love?" Not literally, no. I suggest you consider the dual possibilities in every situation and choose what best suits you. The dark is true in this physical plane just as much as the light is. The key is where you deposit your focus, also known as your faith. Just as you believe a robbery is possible because it just happened to you, believe that justice is simultaneously possible too. Believe in divine intervention. Acknowledge the duality of life, and use it to your benefit; use it to empower you. Believe that just as bad is possible, good is possible too, even in the very moment bad things happen. Your free will always offers you that choice, remember? When darkness fills up your room, believe that you can immediately light up a bright candle and shine away any dark veil. Believe that a robbed item can be replaced in the very moment it was snatched because your birthright is to see good, to see fair, to see love. Either the item will be handed back to you or a better one will be given to you. This is a metaphysical law. Don't focus on the offender; focus on the *truth*. The truth will set you free.

FORGIVENESS

One of the most epic examples of forgiveness was seen in the late Nelson Mandela. He was imprisoned by the oppressive apartheid regime for twenty-seven years. He had to forgive his nation's wrongdoers to be able to transform and bring back peace and a positive change to his beloved country of South Africa. Among his most celebrated quotes are "Forgiveness liberates the soul; it removes fear. That's why it's such a powerful weapon," "Resentment is like drinking poison and hoping it will kill your enemies," and "As I walked out the door toward the gate that would lead to my freedom, I knew that if I didn't leave my bitterness and hatred behind, I'd still be in prison." Such wisdom! He fundamentally understood that by forgiving others, he liberates himself.

Sometimes we think we have forgiven another when we have no clue what it means to really forgive. If you are still blaming someone or something for your current emotional, psychological, or physical baggage, you haven't forgiven yet. When being in the presence of another makes you feel uncomfortable, resentful, or depressed, you have not risen above yet. Whatever negativity another person sparks in you is a negativity you have given life to, and that is for you to heal. The person making you feel that way is only your teacher, and the lesson is always to stay centered no matter what. There are no enemies in this world, only angels in disguise. People are always off the hook. The one carrying the troubled sentiment is the one who hasn't let go of past grudges and the one who will inevitably suffer. You're not giving others a great gift when you finally decide to forgive them. You are giving yourself that great gift, and this is the sweetest, most gratifying gift you can ever give yourself. Forgiveness is another form of love.

You can't say, "I forgave that person long ago; I just don't ever want to see him or her again" or "I forgave them; I just won't forget." Forgiveness takes you back to a state of compassion, acceptance, and unity. It doesn't mean you have to reestablish a relationship that was broken, but as you move on, you must do so with a forgiving heart if you want to really write a new gratifying chapter in your life. If you can think of that person without feeling resentment, rejection, or irritability and if you are able to offer a genuine smile if you bump into the person on the street, then you know you have really forgiven. If you can talk about a certain person without the need to express negative comments about him or her, you have forgiven. Words are thoughts that are charged with powerful manifesting vibration. This is why it has always been said to be careful with your words. They have power. It is incongruent to say, "I have forgiven that person even though he ruined my life." There is no such thing as forgiving someone you still think has ruined a part of your existence. Forgiveness comes with the loving awareness that no one has ever had the power to harm your past, present, or future. Forgiving another means taking responsibility for your own life and feeling grateful for that other person's participation in your life to make you a wiser, stronger, and more compassionate person.

I hear many people complain and blame their families, partners, co-workers, bosses, society, friends, politicians, and even solitude for their misery when they have no one else to blame. They will avoid certain people or situations like the plague, thinking that the distance will save them from their falsely perceived harm. They think that being distant and tight-lipped will honor their pride or that it will dissipate their umbrage, but all they are doing is expanding the unfinished business that will sooner or later have to be addressed with love and compassion. There is no way around this. The universe calls for balance; it is our only duty. If we stray from our center into ego-driven attitudes, life will make sure to bring us back to our essence sooner or later in spite of our resistance. Life has a way of blocking out paths and closing doors we want to open until we cleanse our heart of impurities. A clean heart holds the master key to all the doors of opportunity in this physical realm. In our loving center is where we feel the most peaceful and at home. Our spirit knows this, which is why our spirit is always looking forward to forgive. The only part of us that resists forgiveness is our ego. Forgiving is the only way to exempt the lessons in life. If you have friction with another person, group, relative, or even yourself, consider that friction a test in love that can't be ignored.

START WITH YOUR PARENTS

How wild is it that we begin to build a perception of life in our subconscious mind from the moment we start to develop in the womb? The responsibility of parenthood starts way before the child is born. Whether we know it or not, everything our parents felt, argued, grieved, believed, anticipated, and feared was passed on to us from the moment we were conceived. As soon as we acquired a heartbeat, we became part of our parents' energy field. Sometimes we grow up with certain fears or insecurities we just can't explain. When we finally become aware of what our parents (especially our mothers, who carried us for nine months) were going through, we make sense of so many of our blockages. There are many factors from that past that contributed to the way we currently face life and relate to people. Understanding what our parents felt, thought, or discussed back then can help us build more compassion. This compassionate perspective leads to forgiveness of many things we don't even currently realize we need to forgive, and of course it all starts with Mama and Papa. They were the first two people you had a human interaction (or lack thereof) with. Even if you were given up for adoption the moment you were born, you were still inside your biological mother's womb for nine months, and that mother of yours copulated with your biological father in one way or another to procreate you. Their souls and blood are embedded in you. There is a world of information you inherited from them and is stored in every cell of your being. These subconscious chips of information have been influencing your psyche and beliefs without you even realizing it. Many life obstructions or character barriers that you might currently struggle with have been dragged down from the past, and that's fine. Don't feel discouraged, and don't point the finger, because whatever happened or didn't happen is irrelevant now. If you have the luxury of talking to your parents to find out what the atmosphere was like when you were conceived, birthed, and brought up, then by all means go and learn something new about your origins, and forgive all that wasn't ideal or loving. If you don't have the means of finding out what went on, don't fret. All this valuable information is recorded in your subconscious mind, and if it is too painful or challenging to do the research, start by sitting in silence. Your heart holds all the healing power necessary. All you need is the intention to forgive and let go of any and all blockages you were programmed with from conception. Understanding the true essence of your existence will powerfully exonerate you from the chains of negative subconscious beliefs. Whatever your parents went through during that period of your life does not have to command your behavior. When you fully comprehend that, in spite of it all, you are made of a powerful and shatterproof love, you will find great inspiration to vindicate them of any and all bad judgment that has not allowed you to grow and evolve. You will forgive them, and this will mark a new and promising chapter in your life.

Like I said, sometimes we don't even know that we have some forgiveness work pending in our hearts. I had one of my biggest breakthroughs when I fully understood this concept. The signs are everywhere, but sometimes we go about living our lives with a tunnel vision. If you are struggling with eating disorders, addictions, compulsions, or trust issues; if you don't know how to set barriers for yourself; if you have become an overachiever who feels validation and self-worth only when you accomplish or have gains of some sort; if you feel pressured to look a certain way or to people-please; or if you have trouble saying no, these are all signs of deep insecurities that are rooted in your early years. It is during our prenatal, infancy, and childhood stages that our strong or weak characters and positive or negative belief systems are formed. If we don't tackle these issues by forgiving our parents and ourselves for being subconsciously misled all these years, we will continue living with the same frustrations that can't be healed no matter how good-natured and disciplined in life we are.

Many times we have outstanding relationships with our parents and still struggle with issues from the past that we aren't even aware of. Other times the damage they inflicted on us was very obvious, but we feel like it's in the past and we will never change what happened, so we give up trying to even repair the harm. Whichever the case, every single parent did the very best they could, considering their personal limitations or ignorance. Sometimes they just didn't know any better. Even those who sinned, abandoned, and willfully hurt their kids must have been driven by tremendous personal fear and pain that they were never able to heal themselves. Remember that not everybody heals. So many hurting souls died trying, and that's how they chose to live their lives. Some didn't know any better or were way too stubborn or close-minded to wake up and make positive changes. They missed the point. They never realized they had what it took to live a better life and to be better people, but we can't blame them for this. This is irrelevant to our healing process, and we must not carry their burden in vain. It's time to forgive.

It is probable your parents were afraid if you weren't a planned pregnancy. It is probable they felt shame if they were judged for becoming parents too young, out of wedlock, or what have you. Perhaps when your mother was expecting you, she had to endure abuse or betrayal, and all the fear, loathing, and grief made her experience a sour pregnancy. Maybe she had no support and knew she'd have to raise you on her own and at times even considered abortion, so she was overwhelmingly stressed and felt guilty and ashamed. Many times parents won't admit these things because they don't want to tarnish your perception of the insurmountable love they feel for you, but your subconscious knows better. All the emotions, fears, and beliefs that were processed by the mother during pregnancy are absorbed like a sponge by the baby, so the baby starts to learn about life even before it takes its first breath. Babies inevitably adopt many of the same fears, defense mechanisms, depressive tendencies, and even cravings as their moms!

The learning continues when the baby is a newborn. If it was not fully embraced, for instance, instinct will kick in, and the baby will naturally feel rejected. "Why am I not being held? Am I not good enough?" Being held, rocked, and fed is the biggest source of nourishment and affection that a newborn can receive. This is how a baby starts to get a sense of security and tenderness in life, so when it isn't embraced by its mother, it can instinctively assume it isn't worthy of love. Even if the mother loves the baby deeply but is going through some personal issues, the baby won't understand this rationally, and it will naturally go into defense mode. "If just being born was not enough to receive the proper nourishment from the one I feel most attached to, it must mean that I have to earn this love and affection. If the one I feel safest with won't feed me and care for me, then who will? Am I really safe? Am I really worth it?" This is just the beginning. The effects of this early subconscious programming won't necessarily become apparent until much later in life when the kid grows up and has to learn to become independent and interact with others outside of his or her home.

We then have the father figures and the kids who have to cope with the infamous "Daddy issues." This happens to individuals who had poor fathering, nonexistent fathering, or overfathering cases. If Daddy left when you were little, it is probable that you developed trust issues and subconsciously built a protective wall around yourself. You might have concluded that since the one man who was supposed to protect you and your family never did, how could you ever trust anyone who doesn't have that responsibility over you? Maybe you never got approval from your old man and heard countless times you'd never amount to anything. In any case, one of two things is bound to happen: you either become an overachiever and set extremely high standards for yourself in attempts to prove to Mom and Dad how you are, indeed, worthy of love—or you lose hope and seek solace in other people or in numbing vices to fill the bottomless voids. All emotional turmoil leads to addictions, compulsions, perfectionism, and aggression, among other self-destructive habits that are best intervened with the power of forgiveness. It all starts with healing the wounds of the heart; otherwise, you'll continue running on empty.

For the record, I'm not saying that all perfectionists and overachievers are "damaged goods." First of all, none of us is damaged per se. We're all on a mission to break patterns and set our souls free so that we can say we lived to face life's challenges, overcome, and evolve. No one escapes this because we all face different woes and setbacks to suit our very specific soul's purpose. It can most definitely feel like we are damaged goods, but trust me; you will find many people who are going through a similar circumstance as you, except nobody talks about it openly. We all play the perfection game. The more perfect the better. Even rebellious people who play the "I'm unique in that I'm far from perfect" game are misleading themselves because they are also trying to be as *perfectly imperfect* as possible in attempts to stand out from the rest. We all strive for perfection, and that is fine. It is only when trying to be perfect interferes with our self-esteem and self-worth and affects the way we relate to people that it becomes a problem. Striving for a false sense of perfection can even break relationships and isolate the person with unrealistic standards. Sometimes, as cliché as it sounds, it's good to remember that you are perfect just the way you are. Children who were brought up by parents who weren't too affectionate or communicative might have grown up to think there was something wrong with them and that they had to earn their parent's love, attention, and approval. This is how children start believing they aren't perfect already and become detached from their true, loving essence. Their focus starts to shift outward as they try to figure out what other people are doing to get love, acclaim, acceptance, esteem, and respect and begin obsessing with becoming someone they are not. People stop being themselves or setting healthy boundaries when they try too hard to prove their worth. They stop speaking their truth. They start to please others in spite of their needs. They go on to study medicine because their father is a doctor when all they ever wanted was to be an architect! They settle. They stagnate. They frustrate. They covet. No wonder people love to drink alcohol at social events! It relieves the pressure we live under to be so damn perfect all the time. We fear judgment. We want to loosen up, so we numb ourselves a little to encourage our true selves to come out.

The perfectionist mentality thinks it must achieve something of the extraordinary to be embraced. *Control freaks* fall under this category, as they try to control everything to be perfect. They think they can even control how other people love them. They need to be in command because as children they learned that surrendering to their authentic selves was never enough. In the end, the truth is we are all imperfect, and that's what makes us great and unique. We can't control it all. We can't control people. We can't control circumstances. We need other people's help because we were born to relate. Life happens and people fall in love and out of love, and if things go wrong, it doesn't mean they never loved you or that you can't trust people because they'll dump you for being imperfect. It does not work this way. We must learn to face life's ups and downs without getting rattled inside and losing our self-worth. Remind yourself that the only thing you can control in this lifetime is the way you feel and the way you respect yourself. If others disrespect you, you don't need to blame them; just set healthy boundaries, and wish them well from a distance. No more playing the blame game and trying to manipulate the world. Take responsibility for yourself and forgive.

Forgive your parents. They did the best they could. Their burdens aren't yours any longer. Make amends with them in your heart of hearts. Feel grateful that they gave you this life for you to pursue your dreams and become your best self. Send them light. Apologize for judging them. Don't expect them to be the parents you always idealized. They have always been enough. They have always been perfect for your life plan, as their imperfections have always been part of your divine plan to stop reacting and start forgiving.

BEING RIGHT VERSUS HAVING PEACE

Forgiving is not common in that it has become easier for most people to blame, point the finger, and be right. Sometimes we'd just rather be right than have peace in our hearts. This is where the big *ego versus spirit* fight takes place. We will ardently convince ourselves of the victims we have become, how others did us wrong, how we deserve to be treated right and all we experience is tremendous injustice, how our kids ignore us, how our families don't support us, how our siblings are such monsters, how our friends are so selfish, how our bosses are unfair, how our childhood was so troubled, how our parents abandoned us, how our spouses betrayed us, how our peers rejected us, how our partners robbed us, or how our aggressors stole the best years of our lives or psychologically ruined us. The list goes on. Then we go on telling our story with such righteousness, looking for other people's affirmation of this *truth* we have chosen to adopt and inject life to. We find solace in being told "Poor baby, you are *so right*. How could you endure such selfishness from others? What an unfair life! You must be so hurt. No wonder you are so stuck! How unfortunate." Then we go on digging our holes much deeper, and we wonder why nobody comes to save us or why we can't save ourselves!

First of all, nobody will come to save you. You won't be able to save yourself either, not with a blaming mentality. Nobody is responsible for your irritation, frustration, solitude, or self-destruction but yourself. When you learn to take responsibility for your reality and for the things you are manifesting or lacking, then you will activate real change. Your mission must not be to be right. Your mission must be to find peace in your heart, regardless of the cards that were dealt to you from birth or the cards that are being dealt to you right now. If you even remotely feel like someone else is to blame for your current circumstances, I invite you to practice forgiving yourself for this self-defeating attitude and then go on and forgive those who did you wrong. Yes, they probably did something that triggered an offense, but they didn't make you feel the way you feel. The way you feel is your choice.

The best way to start forgiving is to take your negative feelings, acknowledge where they come from, take responsibility for them, own them, hand them over to God (or to the universe), and replace them with love. Yes, surrender your troubles over to God, and rest assured that it is not, never has been, and never will be up to you to resolve them. Your only responsibility is to *feel love*. Remember that the people who trigger us into feeling negative emotions are messengers. They are messengers of the unhealed parts of ourselves. It is up to us to spot our triggers and inject them with light. It is not enough to think or tell yourself that you have forgiven someone or something. You must feel it, and a great way to feel this love is to have an act of kindness toward the person you are meaning to forgive, even if that means having loving thoughts about them. It all starts in the heart, and the other person does not need to know this. To make yourself feel peace and love in your heart is enough to heal a broken relationship. The other person does not have to agree because what the other person feels or thinks has no power over you unless you allow it to. All that matters is that you train yourself to feel love regardless of what happens outside of yourself and, when you feel the love, continue by spreading it. A heart that flows with love wants to share it with those who are receptive of it. Never forget that forgiving cleanses the heart of blockages and opens it up for love, and open hearts always find each other. As long as you live with an open heart, you will always find someone to love and love you back. Be kind to everyone, even to those who hurt you, because whatever reaction the other person has toward your kindness is absolutely irrelevant. You are not looking for a positive reaction from others but rather for an action of peace in your heart. Always remember that you are blessed with the free will that allows you to choose love over fear in every circumstance of life. Make it a habit to relieve yourself of any burden brought on by others by choosing thoughts of love so that you can walk this earth engulfed in a sphere of clean, bright, magnetic light.

THE EXTRAORDINARY HABIT

Forgiveness sends out a message to the universe that says, "I'm ready. I've grown. I'm healed. Bring it on. Let the good times roll." To forgive has to become a habit that we keep alive with practice. Life will constantly throw challenges at us, and we must be ready to forgive and turn the page. This is what I've seen extraordinary people do time and time again. Developing the habit of forgiving and turning the page can be challenging at first. Your mind will play tricks on you. Your ego will convince you that you can't forgive those who've never given you a break in life. Ego will tell you that you have struggled for so long without support and that you can't trust anyone, but when did you start believing that you had to solve problems on your own? At what point did you decide to revere the idea of struggling? Who told you that you had to fight, and when did you give up help from the biggest supporter in the world? You think you were betrayed and abandoned by everyone to face life's challenges on your own? That is your problem. You have chosen to believe a lie. You have lost your faith, and when you lose faith, you lose strength, you lose vision, and you lose yourself. You have never been alone and never will be. Your biggest savior, supporter, provider, and caregiver is called God, the universe, divine light, higher truth, source, the Holy Spirit, or however you want to call it. God has always been there and always will be. It is only your lack of faith that has troubled you in life and has kept you from forgiving yourself and others for so long.

I have met extraordinary people who, in spite of their upbringings, have forgiven and gone on to build their idea of heaven on earth. I've seen men getting along with their once-wrongdoing peers and wishing well to their once-betraying friends, and they continue to do so because it helps them radiate more light. They know that it is this light that attracts good into their lives anyway, so they are extraordinary in that sense. Ordinary people will tell you to curse those who hurt you and wish them foul. This is one of the most ignorant mentalities ever, but you can't judge the ignorant because, well, they sometimes just don't know any better.

You have to learn and train yourself about how to deal with the negatives in life. You have to learn how to face this life's duality wisely with a forgiving heart because life is made of black and white, and people won't always treat you the way you want to. You can't escape life's polarities and expect to experience only positive, happy-go-lucky happenings. It doesn't work that way. If you keep complaining that only bad things happen to you, it's because you haven't learned how to cope with those things so that they don't irritate you. Obstacles and adversities will keep coming, and you will keep facing them—it's called *life*. The key lies in learning how to control your emotions. This is how you direct the film of your life. You must learn how to transmute negatives into positives, and it all starts in your heart. You have that choice *right now*. You have the option in this moment to hand your troubles and frictions over to God and to surrender to love. This is the key to happiness. Happiness is not only about living only joyful experiences but about learning how to lovingly surrender to negative ones too. The habit of forgiving starts with acknowledging dark emotions; releasing them; trusting that divine justice will take care of any disputes; and replacing fear, worry, and grief with optimism, faith, and gratefulness. This is how you bring yourself back to peace. This is the only lesson to be learned amid unnerving situations. Even if a person who did you wrong failed to apologize, you can practice forgiving him or her because that is all it takes to heal relationships. Closure is established through forgiveness.

Stop expecting others to please or praise you. You have to be at ease in spite of everyone else's behavior because you can't control what people do. Try to look beyond betrayals or attacks, and make it a habit to consider other people's actions as divine moves orchestrated by God to better suit your divine plan. Don't fret, don't cling to people, don't cling to jobs, don't cling to properties, let everything go, and let life be. It is in your best interest to forgive and observe whatever changes occur before your eyes because everything is constantly changing. Blaming is a waste of valuable energy that can be ideally preserved in stillness and observation. Train your heart to be at ease with whatever people decide to say, do, or not do, and learn to listen to yourself instead. If your gut feeling is telling you to distance yourself from certain people and get closer to those who have a positive aura to them, do it. Your higher self knows what's best for you, so don't ignore the messages of your soul. Spirit will always guide you in the right direction of a higher frequency, and you don't need to mingle with those who want to vibrate lower than you. Don't be afraid to let go of toxic people to walk a more promising path, and don't ever feel lonely because you're not.

You are never alone. God is always orchestrating everything from above. In the end, if you are in disagreement with another person's way of life or beliefs, it does not mean you have to hold grudges against him or her. Forgiveness is also about respect and not making other people's words or behavior your own. Whatever someone else says or does has absolutely nothing to do with you, even if their sentences begin with your name. Nothing is ever personal except in that it is trying to teach you compassion and forgiveness and to set you free. There need not be any friction, tension, or resentment toward another who might be trying to pull you down to his or her same negativity. If someone showed up in your life to disrupt your peace, all you have to do is consider them a lesson in love to practice compassion. Consider them a cue to express your greatness by treating them with respect. Consider them a neglected side of yourself that seeks acceptance, and then release them. You don't have to stick around darkness; you just have to forgive it, bless it, and release it. Splitting and walking away from gloomy people or situations is not tragic at all if it protects your light. Part of respecting yourself is setting healthy boundaries and making sure your heart is always getting a refill of uplifting experiences by situating yourself in loving atmospheres and surrounding yourself with loving people.

Many times we fear letting go of toxic relationships because we don't trust that we will find more loving bonds, but this is a lie. Don't ever feel like you're alone in your quest. Your higher self will always pair you up with your same resonance, so be brave enough to feel good and wait for more goodness to find you. Don't ever feel like you have no support because you always, at every second, have the biggest, most powerful support anyone could ever have, and that is God. He will take care of you. He will remain by your side all throughout your life. God is indeed your most loving companion, and if you are ready to start sharing your life with another human being, all you have to do is tell God you are ready. He will make sure to keep showering you with love through the physical presence of others. God shows up in the form of other people as well. All of a sudden, someone will cross your path, and it won't be an accident or because you got lucky. You have not been lonely because of bad luck or bad karma. If you really want to share your life with other like-minded people, you ask God to give you that gift, and he will. Sooner or later, you'll meet someone, and it will be a product of your good faith, surrendering, and trusting in the process of forgiving, letting go, and staying present to allow new blessings to enter your life.

HAPPY SOULS ATTRACT HAPPY THINGS

You do you, hon. Whatever happens with anyone out there, in the end it's best to remember that it all starts with you. Wish everyone well, no matter what, because happy people do happy things and make other people happy too. If you cleanse your soul of negative thoughts and heavy grudges, you will have risen above your ego and liberated yourself. It matters not what others think, say, or do. It matters not if others have met you halfway on your path to forgiveness. It matters not if others have been or have not been receptive to your healing. All that matters is that you find positive, yummy feelings in your core when you check in with your heart. The only thing that's important is that you can think of anyone out there and hope they are doing well and wish everyone much love and success, because love attracts love.

Ask yourself what triggers you. Figure out what makes you react, and make it your mission to reform those parts of yourself that are weak and insecure. Whatever friction you have with another is never about what he or she did or said to you but entirely about how you perceive yourself. If whatever somebody else does makes you react defensively, it does not necessarily mean that the person's comments or actions were offensive, or maybe those words and actions remind you on a subconscious level of a personal insecurity or fear you have not resolved yet. Maybe you don't feel confident enough to make your own decisions and stand your own ground, so those remarks may feel like a pressure bomb that makes you explode. Sometimes the best dialogue is the one we hold with ourselves. To dig deep in our subconscious minds to learn about what triggers us can help us forgive ourselves and forgive others more easily. Know yourself and spot your unresolved, blocking insecurities. Effective dialogue does not happen when you tell another person how *he or she* made you feel. Real dialogue takes place only when you put your guard down and approach the other person to tell him or her how *you* allowed him or her to make you feel and that you are looking for peace of mind and love over anything else. This is mature. In the end, you must take care of you; it is up to nobody else to make you feel better.

Strive to be the bigger person in any disagreement with someone else, and have a compassionate approach to resolving issues. It helps to allow your emotions to cool off and speak with a collected mind instead of letting your impulsive self address any situation. In the end, anger and aggression may seem protective because they inject energy to an argument, but this energy is negative. It takes a calm mind to have a wise perspective and come up with real solutions. Both forgiving and apologizing are simultaneous acts. When you apologize to another, you are forgiving yourself for having held him or her responsible for your feelings, just as when you forgive another, you are apologizing to yourself for initially holding grudges against him or her.

Even when somebody hurts us and we do in fact deserve an apology, having the person say "I'm sorry" is not the thing that will heal us, as good as having them apologize feels. Real healing happens when we find love in our hearts regardless of what the other person says or does. You must also be ready to accept that sometimes dialogue won't be possible if your counterpart isn't riding the same compassionate wave you are, and that is fine too. All that matters is that you cleanse yourself of all negative feelings. How else will you make wise decisions if you aren't even aware of what emotional turmoil is taking place in your heart? We must always tap into our feelings so that we can bring them to our awareness and make amends with ourselves, no matter what. If we don't externalize, our emotions eventually stagnate, crystallize, and disease us.

Sometimes the people we want to forgive or apologize to aren't alive anymore or will be far away and distanced from us. Other times it will happen that we just don't have the fluidity in words to dialogue. In this case I recommend writing apology letters. Think of all the people you have had friction with in the past. Scan your heart for any pending remorse, resentment, hate, or regrets, and write them down as an apology letter. A very important thing to consider is that an apology letter is *not* an anger-venting letter. The heart is made of love, not of anger. If you write a letter that you intend to have someone else read, make sure it contains no angry content. You can't tell someone, "I forgive you, but keep in mind how much you hurt me" or "I am sorry, but what you did to me was truly unfair." That is *not* forgiving or apologizing. Ultimately, you want this letter to help *you* heal, not another. In order to heal, you will have to really own your feelings and want nothing more than to feel peace, love, and respect for yourself and others.

I was once terribly hurt by someone, and instead of eternally waiting for his apology, I decided to write him an apology letter instead. Yes, I myself apologized for taking an active part in our conflict and for whatever negativity I made him feel too. I was sorry for not being strong enough to walk away on good terms, and I was sorry for allowing my ego-charged resentment and remorse to take over and stay prevalent all the time after we parted ways. I was sorry for judging him. I knew that holding on to judgment, blame, and resentment was only poisoning me, and I didn't need that baggage anymore. I was ready to say, "I'm sorry" even if the other person did me wrong or ignored my apology. I understood that in any friction, it takes two to tango. I sent the letter to that person and never got a response. I never heard back from him, and we never had the closure I would have loved to have, but something bigger and better happened. I finally felt peace in my heart from the moment I finished writing that letter. Every time I thought of this individual, I felt nothing but gratefulness and warmth in my heart. The person had given me the opportunity to practice forgiveness and heal wounds. This, in and of itself, breaks negative life patterns too.

RELEASE YOUR GUILT

Forgiving yourself means letting go of your guilt. Many people carry much guilt under the surface, and it eats at them more and more each time. There's a myriad of things we can feel guilty about and not even know it. One thing to keep in mind when playing this game called life is that there is only one rule: *only you are responsible for yourself.* Knowing this can free you of built-up guilt. Parents are not responsible for their children, children are not responsible for their parents, spouses are not responsible for each other, and friends aren't to be held accountable for one another either. To assume responsibility and look out for another human being is a magnificent act of love and generosity that is very much part of our human nature, but nobody is obliged to care for another when they aren't ready, suited, or compelled to do so, and there is no sin in that. Surrender your guilt once and for all. Let go of whatever you could have done, should have done, or would have done in the past. Everything that happened before happened in a perfect way and for a divine reason. It had to be that way, and there's no point in accumulating more guilt over it. It is what it is. You live and you learn. If you weren't the greatest parent, you did the best you could. If you weren't the kindest partner, you didn't consciously mean any harm. Sometimes our subconscious takes over, and we do things our hearts don't necessarily mean to do, but it's all part of the learning process, and apologizing and forgiving from the heart is good enough. Being human means we are not perfect. We are all a work in progress, and learning to release our guilt and forgive ourselves is part of that learning process. You weren't born knowing it all, and nobody handed you a life manual, because there isn't one, so cleanse your heart of any and all guilt. Your life starts now because now always offers a clean slate.

GENEROSITY

The heart wants to give. Our nature is to serve, convey, and contribute. We live under the impression that receiving is the biggest gift, but if you reflect upon this, there is no greater pleasure in life than giving and serving others. The very purpose of our lives is to leave behind a legacy. Nobody wants to pass on thinking that they made no difference in this lifetime. We long to make a change. We are always trying to come up with ideas of how to attain self-realization so that we can feel proud and accomplished, but there is no sense of accomplishment if our efforts don't affect others. Others are meant to mirror back at us how we thrive. Just like doctors save lives, lawyers defend the innocent, artists stimulate audiences, and athletes prove to us what we are physically capable of, we all want to practice something that serves humanity in one way or another. Our impact in this world is measured by how many lives we touch, help, and inspire. Everything we aspire to do means nothing to us if it does not influence our peers. For this very same reason, we must not forget how valuable we are. Each and every one of us was born with a unique gift that no one else can match. Even if we don't see it yet, we must find that which we were born to contribute to without comparing ourselves to the rest. The world needs your gift; otherwise, you would not be breathing. Your existence is not in vain; it is perfectly planned for a big contribution, and all contributions are equally significant.

Some people have huge bank accounts to donate funds to charities, while others have big companies to offer jobs to the unemployed, but to those of you who aren't tycoons, moguls, or business owners, your time and presence are worth millions too. They say time is money. Cash money can be regenerated or reclaimed, but your time is priceless. Your time, once used up, is practically irreplaceable. Very often your time can be more valuable than currency, which is why people frequently say, "Thank you for taking your time." It is a big donation and shows great generosity. If you ever feel like you have nothing to give, think again. You have the luxury of reaching out to someone to offer a helping hand in whichever way possible. We always think that the one thing people need to solve their problems is money, but sometimes what they would really benefit from is good company, good advice, moral support, and to feel they aren't alone in their struggles. "Money doesn't buy happiness" is such a cliché phrase, but how many people with fat bank accounts feel so poor at the same time? Money isn't the only valuable token. Offering your time is just as generous.

When it comes to generosity and the whole idea of giving and receiving, it is safe to say that you don't have to wait to fill up your piggy bank before you can help another economically or that you have to wait to become such and such a professional before you can receive a much-needed flow of income. You don't have to become something other than what you already are to be deserving of prosperity and abundance. All these blockages exist only in your head, which give you an experience that feels so real, but as we just mentioned, reality is not as you perceive it. Reality happens at very subtle levels. You must replace all your old belief systems with the ones that serve you. You don't have to cheat, steal, lie, judge, worry, blame, or have enemies, because you already have it all, and no one is robbing you of what you want to have. The collective consciousness is always reading your vibrational resonance to create your next moment.

You want to make sure that the next moment brings fairness, friendship, honesty, health, love, and respect, so you act in accordance with that. This is where the phrases "You get what you give," "What goes around comes around," "Do unto others as you would have them do unto you," "You sow what you reap," "As above so below," and so on come from. Your acts will define your next moment. Your next moment is now.

THE BEST THINGS IN
LIFE ARE FREE

You were born wealthy. That you have to go out into the world and acquire all the things you believe will make you happy is a distorted belief. Material possessions and currency gains naturally flow into the lives of those who feel rich, and if some were born into material wealth before even understanding what currency means, it is simply because many of their most important life lessons revolve around other issues than figuring out how to build their economy. It means nothing. All life lessons are equally important and weigh the same in the balance of spirit, so we can't go around comparing and feeling less or more fortunate than the rest. In the end, we are all an intricate part of each other. A collective consciousness affects our individual life purpose so that we, as a whole, can benefit from the victories and evolution of all humankind. We can't judge books by their covers. A person with millions of dollars in his or her bank account might go to sleep with worries of another nature, such as health concerns, family feuds, rejection, phobias, loneliness, a bad reputation, or addictions.

Yes, currency can buy many things that make our lives convenient, but convenience is not the real source of our happiness. The best things in life are indeed free. Why am I even talking about wealth? Simply because it is something that many people believe they lack and thus live in pursuit of. They won't feel worthy or loved until they achieve material wealth, so they never find a fluffy pillow to rest their heads on at night because they exhaust their minds trying to figure out how to build wealth. They forget that they have permanent access to a well of abundant wealth within them.

The biggest source of wealth is the heart. Think about it. Our external realities are nothing more than a reflection of the heart's state of affairs. We don't need currency to get our hands on the things that bring us real joy, bliss, and contentment. Yes, I might want to travel afar to learn about different cultures and live new experiences. Therefore, my main goal might be to gather the necessary funds to travel the world, but if I don't have such funds in this very moment, I must remember that there's a divine reason for it! It might be that the soul's desire is that I come up with new ideas of making money because in that process I might gain the insight, experience, and valuable knowledge that I might have never gathered if I had just been given the funds without effort on my part. There's always a hidden opportunity in every challenge. The latter phrase is not a cliché.

Enjoying the journey more than arriving at the destination is what life is all about. Think about the times you accomplished something and how, were it not for the journey, the goal itself wouldn't have tasted as sweet. So what is better and richer than high-end clothes, expensive travel, luxury cars, jewels, and large properties? Well, how about perfect health, loyal friendships, intimacy, a loving partner, freedom, movement, and creative expression? You most definitely don't need cash to get fit and feed your body mindfully. You don't need a credit card to build honest friendships and attract loyal partners who support you in your journey. You don't have to write a check to purchase the right to express yourself through exercising, dancing, writing, or entertaining. No one will charge you to help others, which in and of itself can bring you huge satisfaction as well. These are the things that really fill up your cup. These are things without which you would truly get to experience a void that's impossible to fill with diamonds and pearls.

The beauty of it all is that you have access to these blessings right about now. Even if you are currently facing challenge and adversity in your life, these are the God-given gifts that will help you pull through any obstacle thrown your way, and it is your responsibility to make use of them. You are responsible for your happiness. Playing the victim is an immature way of trying to find comfort, because you do have a way out in any tough life scenario. You always have the tools to get yourself out of a rut, and they are free. You have talent, vision, imagination, creativity, gratitude, intuition, faith, and compassion. You have love. You have a heart. Make use of it. Your heart has more purchase power than an AMEX Black Centurion Card.

Material wealth is indeed fabulous. Yes, it can make life so much easier, enjoyable, and interesting which is why we covet and desire it and daydream of it. I always encourage people to feel proud of longing to be rich if that is what they visualize for themselves. I am a proponent of honoring your aspirations and ambitions no matter what. Money is a facilitator of many things, so it is only natural that we work hard for it. The thing to remember is just that a hefty bank account is not and will not become the source of your happiness, ever. You must know this, or you will be painfully awakened to a higher truth sooner or later.

Some people with a lower net worth than others are much richer and live much more satisfactory lives because they depend on the only permanent source of wealth, which is their heart. It is an infallible law of physics that those who are wealthy in spirit eventually attract physical wealth anyway because we attract who we are, not what we want.

I fell in love with an answer from Russian president Vladimir Putin when asked if he was really one of the richest men in the world as many speculated. The film director Oliver Stone was interviewing him, and Mr. Stone started by saying, "I know I would have a hell of a lot more fun if I was rich," to which Mr. Putin responded, "You know, I do not think that is what brings great happiness. With this crisis, you would be thinking about what to do with your assets, how to save them, and where to place them. It would only bring you headaches. You are far wealthier than those who have great wealth in their accounts. You have an opinion of your own, you have a talent, you have a chance to show this talent, and you have a chance to leave a great legacy behind. Money doesn't bring this kind of happiness. Because when you are in a coffin, you don't have any pockets to take your money to the grave with you" (Oliver Stone, *The Putin Interviews*. Showtime, 2017). What a centered mentality. In the end, one thing is for sure: the happiest man is not the man who has it all but the one who needs the least.

LAWS OF ATTRACTION, CAUSE AND EFFECT

Your generosity is not all tangible. You are always giving in the form of energy as well. Your contributions are packed with a powerful, creative force. If you give someone a sum of money, that money has purchasing power. If you give someone a lending hand, that act is made of cooperative power. If you give someone your time, that carries presence power. When you offer a smile to another, your smile is charged with heartening power. Your good advice has uplifting power. If what you give is criticism, then you are sending out offensive power and so on. These power-packed actions work like magnets because we live in an electromagnetic field. Whatever energy you cast out into the universe will adhere to more energy like it and attract it back to you. This is how we subconsciously manipulate what we receive, and this is what explains the phrase "Giving is receiving." The quality of the energy you radiate out to the universe through your actions will activate a similar reaction. Like attracts like. In other words, if your actions are packed with generous, kind, loving energy, you will receive generous, kind, and loving experiences. This is a universal law; there is no way around it. I know what you're thinking: "So if like attracts like, then why do opposites attract?" I'm glad you're paying attention.

Please let me give you a little physics crash course just so that you can fully grasp this metaphysical concept of giving and receiving, cause and effect. Every physical and nonphysical thing in this universe is made of *energy*, but only the physical things are made of *elements* (air, earth, wood, water, fire). When people ask, "If like attracts like, then why do opposites attract?" the answer is very simple. Like attracts like at an energetic level. Beliefs are made of energy, emotions are made of energy, and thoughts are made of energy, so people who share similar beliefs, feelings, and thought patterns will inevitably find each other. On the other hand, opposites attract only at an elementary level. Two opposing elements can share the same energy, and this is why they attract each other. This is the case when an aggressive person attracts a submissive one. The aggressor and the victim look so physically different and act in such physically opposing ways, but they both share identical metaphysical (energetic, nonphysical) beliefs. The aggressor believes in abusing and attacking, while the submissive believes in being abused and being attacked. *Bingo.* They're made for each other, energetically speaking. Energy is at the core of everything that is compatible or incompatible, for that matter. Whether two subjects are opposites or alike on a physical level is irrelevant given we are essentially big bundles of energy responding and eternally orchestrating on an electromagnetic-field level. It is in this electromagnetic field where like attracts like, so we better make sure that we give out the same energy quality that we wish to receive.

It is common to hear people say, "What you give is what you get," and this of course is meant in a broader sense. You attract people, places, and things that allow you to meet your soul's purpose. You will get whatever your energy is attracting back to you. Your energy will always fish for things that help you get closure on a specific issue that was left unsolved or to reenact something from the past that wants to be acknowledged and felt. Whatever you reject or resent might not be what you consciously want to face, but your subconscious knows better, and it is ultimately your subconscious that makes up the quality of your energy. Your subconscious is the side of you that desperately wants to heal, so it will relentlessly keep attracting people and situations that will help you come to terms with pending psychological and emotional wounds left hurting. In this sense, your soul is naturally generous in that it is always providing you with the things that will help you rise and overcome. Healing opportunities are all around you all the time because every single element that makes up your physical reality was wisely called on by you to help you grow and achieve. If you just pay close attention and become aware of your surroundings, you can have constant breakthroughs. Your life's treasures are not just in the sweet, joyful things you experience but also in the trials and tribulations. The things that you resist, the things that make you mad, and the things that make you act defensive are diamonds in the rough. The anxiety you want to numb and the remarks from others that hurt you are showing you the face of your past trauma, blockages, and scarred wounds. These things that bother you the most are the things that desperately want to be felt, forgiven, and released once and for all to be able to heal.

Energy is forever wise and will always pair up with other energies out there that complement it perfectly to serve a higher purpose. If the introverted you are keenly attracted to someone else's dynamic energy, it is probably because you are ready to expand your self-expression. All in all, if you are strongly attracted to another person, it simply means both of your souls are eagerly ready to clear blockages (opposites attract) or validate similarities (like attracts like). In relationships that bring chaos and challenge, both souls are looking to reenact unresolved patterns so that they can bring them to consciousness and transform them with compassion and forgiveness. This is the only way to clear blockages and mend broken hearts. In the end, people will come and go. The ones who stay are the ones who balance themselves out at the same rhythm we do, and the ones who take a different route do so because they no longer share the frequency of our energetic field, and that is perfect too. When two people part ways, it does not necessarily mean that love is lost but rather that their magnetic fields don't share a common purpose anymore, and that is perfectly fine.

I find it extremely fascinating that, when it comes to universal laws, absolutely everything is legal and just. All things are essentially fair because they are all perfectly synchronized and paired up by the universal law of cause and effect. Universal laws, also known as metaphysical laws, are infallible and indisputable. What you give is what you get. There's no injustice ever because you set the frequency of your physical reality through your thoughts, feelings, and actions, and it is this frequency that attracts whatever matches it to give you a fairly congruent life experience.

SENDING PEOPLE LIGHT

When we see somebody else struggling, and we feel impotent to their suffering because we can't buy them freedom, health, or happiness, how do we help them? What do we do when even our time is of no use to them? It is somewhat common to tell the person that we will keep them in our prayers and that we will send them much light and loving thoughts. I bet you these people think, "Gee, thanks, you might as well just wish me good luck." Do you really understand how praying for someone or sending them much light can be a generous act? How will it ever make a difference to express our good wishes if we don't feel an ounce of faith that our bona fide thoughts alone can help at all? Many people wish others well in their thoughts but don't have real faith in their hearts that their good wishes alone will create an impact whatsoever.

The fact that you can perceive a person fighting for his or her life or another one struggling with debt is only possible because they are in divine alignment with you. You would not be able to perceive their reality if their reality wasn't linked to yours on an energetic, spiritual level. When you tell people you will pray for them and that you will "send them much light," it does not mean that you will literally put a ray of light in an envelope and deliver it to their mailbox. Sending light or offering prayer practically means that you will focus and deposit your faith on the positive side of the spectrum of whatever negativity they are experiencing. If they are ill, you will focus on their health. If they are broke, you will focus on their wealth. If they are lonely, you will focus on their companionship. By directing your focus to all that is good, abundant, and loving for others, you basically affirm, uphold, and support that very same reality for your own perception. Whatever happens to others is indirectly and simultaneously happening to you. Their struggle is surfacing hopeless, sad, or irritable emotions in you, so you subconsciously try to find a way to transmute these feelings into positive ones for you to find your own relief. All of a sudden, it is in your best interest that they heal so that you can rid yourself of the pain it causes you to witness their struggle. You offer them help so that you can relieve your perception.

How would you help yourself in their shoes? What if one of the most powerful and generous things you could do for them would be to sit in silence and use your imagination to activate positive change? If you take their misfortune, mentally adopt it for a few minutes, and meditate on how you would change your beliefs and thinking patterns if you were them so as to manifest the best outcome for yourself, you might be on to something very powerful. When you take their reality, make it your own in your mind, and change the belief patterns that you know will activate positive change, then you can rest assured you've given them one of the most generous contributions ever. That is what "sending them light" is all about. You decide that you don't believe in their suffering, so you visualize them in perfect health; you visualize them abundant, accompanied, successful, relieved, fluent, and graceful, and then you let it go. Your good energy alone will get to work in supporting their cause. The fact that you don't focus on their suffering anymore means you stop cooperating with their negative cause, which in turn will help to heal both of your perceptions. Sooner or later your positive perception of them will energetically affect their reality and help break their chains as well as yours because you won't share their pain anymore. When sending light to others, don't wait to see results either. Don't cling to or pressure the natural flow of life. You must let go and let God get to work. Your only responsibility is to have a positive perception of people and of life. Don't believe me? Try it, and believe it yourself.

EVERYTHING IS AN ILLUSION

All that you perceive with your five senses is not really there. People and objects seem very real because they are all made up of eternally dynamic energy that bounces around at infinite speeds taking different forms depending on our focus. They feel real because we can see, hear, touch, and smell them, but in truth they exist only through our perception. The bountiful energy that makes up this infinite universe takes on the shape, size, taste, and smell we are ready to experience when we are ready to experience it. It is merely your perception of things that brings them to life in a way that, if you shift your focus, they cease to exist. Since we are constantly holding a perception of things, they seem to constantly be there, but in truth they are not. This explains Einstein's theory that there is no such thing as time and space. We have a perception of time and space, but it is nothing more than creative energy manifesting itself into different forms at the speed of light. We think that days come and go, that time passes, and that we grow old, but what is really happening is that we are playing out the concept of day, night, new, and old that we hold in our minds. We believe in time, so we experience time. Our senses make this physical experience feel so real for a very important reason. We need to feel like our time here is limited so that we find the motivation to get to work. The universe has everything perfectly planned out to benefit our spiritual evolution. How would you feel encouraged to make a change if you had unlimited time to procrastinate? Why would you want to influence others if everyone had a perfect existence? Knowing that life is nothing but energy in motion empowers us because it helps us to stop obsessing with the past and stop anticipating the future. It all happens now, and whatever happens now is a product of your perception. You have the power to make a change in your world by simply shifting your focus and injecting more energy into the things you want to manifest instead of feeding more manifesting energy to the things that trouble you.

Whatever you can imagine already exists. If you don't see it manifested in your current physical reality, it just means it is vibrating in a parallel universe. The linear life we experience moving from past to present to future is not linear in movement at all. Our physical senses just make us feel like we come from somewhere and like we are going somewhere, but in truth we are just happening right here all the time. The things we focus on enter our reality and participate in our present moment. We sense that things happened yesterday or that they are bound to happen tomorrow, but it all happens right now because now is all there is. This is why it's so powerful to *know* that whatever you desire or believe is already real and happening as we speak. If you place your focus on what you want with full certainty of its existence, you call it into your reality and experience it with all your five senses. Think of it as the films we get to enjoy at the movie theater. On screen we get to watch a story in continuous movement, and it looks very real. Nobody wants to be told that the movement they see is not real because it would ruin their experience, but what is actually happening is that they are watching a filmstrip that contains many individual frames with still images. These individual frames are being presented at very high rates of speed, one after the other, creating the experience of life in movement that appears very real, but there is no such thing. It is all an illusion. In the very same way, our physical realities are set up so that we experience them from moment to moment because that is all there is: one moment. The continuity of slight changes we experience is happening at infinite speeds, which is why we feel like we are in movement, but this motion is just an illusion. We are experiencing a series of parallel realities all the time. We jump from one parallel reality to another, and this dynamic is fueled by our personal vibration.

Remember that our vibration is determined by our thought patterns, beliefs, and emotions. In truth, you get to physically experience only a very small percentage of what is out there. The other big chunk of reality that you can't see is made up of what we call spirit, collective consciousness, God, universe, divine energy, and so on. This spiritual consciousness is so bountiful, generous, and loving that it is always holding your hand and guiding you into the next parallel reality that matches your mental makeup. Spirit wants to give you what you want all the time, so it pays close attention to your beliefs and thoughts so that it can take you to that very specific parallel reality that matches them. This way you get to fully experience whatever your focus has decided to focus on, and thus you are always living in perfect fairness and justice to what your core beliefs are. In other words, if you are feeling grateful, optimistic, and loving, your very intelligent spirit will take you to the already-existing parallel reality that is in perfect alignment with your last moment of being grateful, loving, and joyful. You jump from one existing moment to another. Nothing is ever created because everything already exists. Moments just feel *new* because we transition from one moment to another all the time based on our beliefs, but all moments already exist. We just focus on them and experience them simultaneously in the *now*. In a sense, the Holy Spirit is acting very much like a mirror. It is just showing you what you are already made of. Life is nothing but a series of perceptions. Like I said before, you are the director of your life movie.

YOU CREATE YOUR REALITY

When I realized that spirit is always giving me what I focus on, I decided to make many changes to my belief patterns. I even had to dig deep to pluck out the hidden beliefs that were operating from my mind's subconscious level. This sounds like a very complicated process that can only be accomplished in a psychiatrist's office or by purchasing costly hypnotic therapy sessions. Some people go to more extreme measures and take hallucinogenic drugs to get altered states of consciousness in the search for clarity and sanity. People sometimes think that this vast subconscious ocean of answers is so inaccessible that they feel helpless trying to figure themselves out on their own. I'm here to tell you that you have the power to heal your perspective right now by taking your own initiative and achieving quantum leaps of growth by your own efforts. Deciphering yourself is not meant to be a complicated, long, or confusing struggle. Signs and aids are all around you because your life's principal aim is to surround you with healing opportunities. Therapy starts by bringing into your awareness all the things you have an issue with. You must learn to get comfortable with your uncomfortable. You must embrace sobriety and mindfulness so that you can tap into the deepest layers of your consciousness and shine a light on the depths of your soul that have been locked up in the dark for so long. You don't need stimulants, sedatives, hallucinogens, or allopathic medicines to get access to the deepest levels of your being because you are equipped to heal on your own. That is how your divinely perfect body is connected to your mind and soul. The body can naturally heal itself through mindful awareness and surrender. All the parts of our being that we have been resisting will show their faces as we delve deeper into ourselves. We have been conditioned from childhood, we have been traumatized, we have acquired destructive habits along the way, we have adopted limiting beliefs, we have attached ourselves to certain ideas and people, and we have collected our fair share of fears along the way. All these layers of negativity make up the shadow that constantly follows us everywhere we go, and this shadow wants nothing more than to be acknowledged, felt, forgiven, and embraced. Our shadow will never heal if we keep judging it, condemning it, or being ashamed of it. It wants to step into the spotlight, even if for a second, so that it can get showered with healing light once and for all. All our past traumas that made us bitter, fearful, resentful, shy, anxious, and cynical are playing a huge role in our present moment because they are charging the frequency of our energy from a subconscious level. When you finally realize that the quality of your energy is pulling into your experience more of the same frequency-matching moments, you wake up and start to make a change! It's a very wise thing to do. As a matter of fact, it is the *only* thing to do if you want to transform and experience new and improved realities. People never change; they transform. Your essence can't change because you are a spiritual being of love, abundance, and joy. The only thing you can change is the polarity of your thoughts from negative to positive, but your essence always stays the same. Face your life with full consciousness. The only way to create your own reality is to stop being intimidated by the external flow of events. There are absolutely no threats out there, only healing opportunities. Whatever people say, do, or don't do should be of no concern to you. If you are ticked off by other people's actions, then you will have found a powerful mirror that wants to show you a hidden layer of yourself that needs to be felt and loved. People are nothing more than mirrors. They are angels sent from heaven not only to shower us with love but also to help us face the most painful sides of ourselves. We would never be able to tap into the depths of our souls if it weren't for the way we see ourselves in others. Our perceptions of others hold all the pieces of our puzzles.

INTIMACY AS A GENEROUS ACT

In terms of loving relationships, there is nothing more beautiful you can give your spouse or partner than your authenticity. When you understand that no one is out to harm you because you yourself are defining your moment-to-moment experience on this earth, then you put your guard down and start trusting the process of life as it unfolds. To be yourself all the time is a very generous act, given your uniqueness is practically your biggest contribution to the world. You can trust everyone because you are always being loved by God. You have nothing to fear and much to look forward to. There are people who are so unbelievably hesitant to ever admit that they are afraid. They think that admitting they are afraid will make them seem weak, so they put on a brave mask. They want people to think of them as resilient and indestructible warriors because God forbid they judge them as weak for ever feeling scared. This all happens subconsciously, by the way. These people developed a belief that they couldn't trust anyone but themselves and that to be vulnerable can end in humiliation, betrayal, or disapproval. It's like the kid who open-heartedly tells his parents that he loves them and gets the stink eye in return or the kid who shares her feelings and is made fun of. These children grow up building a strong barrier around them because their experience taught them that to be vulnerable was too painful. They trust no one. They fear much. They won't admit it. Why would they? They have convinced themselves that it's safer to put on a strong face and shield themselves from further harm. What's sad is that deep inside of them lives a beautiful, powerful, and healing heart that wants to express its authenticity and is not being allowed to, so the person suffers and doesn't even know why. Their hearts are aching to be seen and understood. They are aching to be brave enough to allow themselves to feel pain, but they don't do it because they haven't learned that they can manage pain without shutting their hearts down and that whatever they feel is beautiful and healing, not threatening. Everything feels like a threat for them. People eat to fill up these voids and then get so obese because fat is symbolically working as that protective shield they so desperately cling to. It doesn't have to be this way. To be vulnerable can heal many wounds. Being vulnerable is a courageous and generous act that all our loved ones get to enjoy and benefit from, not just us. In this sense, to allow ourselves to be vulnerable is one of the most giving acts we can offer another.

Being vulnerable doesn't just mean that you allow yourself to be seen shedding a few tears. Being vulnerable also consists of trusting everyone and not living in defense mode. A lack of intimacy is sometimes linked to not believing that one is genuinely loved. Some people feel like their partner loves exclusively what they can take from them, but that love in and of itself is not real. Deep inside they doubt that they are being loved for them, so they live paranoid all the time. They have an ingrained false belief that tells them they are easily replaceable, so they never fully surrender to love or let go. Intimacy is all about loving and letting go. When one doubts, one keeps up a shield, and a shield never allows for intimacy. Keep in mind that to be intimate with another is one of the most loving, creative, and generous acts one can offer. Allow yourself to really put your guard down and trust that you have nothing to fear because people are your compassionate mirrors to help you heal, not your enemies.

GOD'S GOT YOUR PAYCHECK

Optimism pays. When you decide to take responsibility for your life circumstances, define your goals, forgive, surrender your problems to God, focus on giving, and make it your most important job to transmute your negative feelings into good ones, you'll find yourself in the most lucrative position that God's Company (a.k.a. the universe) can offer. If things aren't going exactly as you planned or if life throws unexpected and disheartening events at you, remember that they are all there to make you better, wiser, stronger, and a more solid human being. Life is always preparing you for what's next. You are always preparing yourself for what's next. You might not know this consciously, but metaphorically speaking you have signed an agreement contract with God's company endorsing absolutely everything that occurs to you—the good and the bad. Be grateful for everything that happens to you because it is there to enrich you. You chose it. No blaming, remember? Count to ten and *act*; don't react.

Many people find relief in complaining. It can sometimes be cathartic, as complaining is a form of venting that opens the floodgates to built-up emotions. If you are going to complain, I recommend you do it in a journal. Write it out. Nobody wants to hear things that you probably just need to spit out as a form of release and spiritual detox. Unless they are your close-knit friends, family, or trained professionals like counselors or psychologists, complaining is best kept private. Friends and family can be there to pat you on the back and understand where you come from, but even friends and family don't have the answers and can sometimes give out detrimental advice that confuses and sinks you further. I don't mean to isolate you, but when it comes to answers and feeling better, it's best you train to pick yourself back up without letting too many others interfere. You have your wisest answers within because you have been crafting this life plan yourself. Make it a habit to tap into your core and decipher where you come from, where you stand, and where you want to go next. If talking to people helps, then do it, but only consult with those who know you well and genuinely care for you. As you fish for answers within yourself, make sure to stay mindful, engage only in acts of love, and trust that all is well and that you are bound to come out of any situation a stronger person. Avoid the blame game, abstain from numbing yourself, stay present, and focus on your next wise move without ever hurting others because karma will always come to bite you in the rear end.

Your biggest legacy is to become the best version of yourself. Amen. The collective consciousness wants you to succeed. It is of no use to lament yourself. It is a waste of energy to resent people even if they directly participated in or perpetuated the adversity you currently face. You hired them! Think of it that way: in spirit, you signed them up for this one. You need them to keep strengthening your forgiveness skills and to sharpen your sense of responsibility, so don't resent anyone involved. You need those virtues to become an extraordinary and noteworthy giant. Stay tolerant, patient, and faithful that before you know it, all you ever set your mind to accomplish will come to be, not one minute early and not one minute late. In God's perfect timing, you will be absolved from your own traps, and you will understand that everything happened how it was meant to happen for you to evolve.

Be clear about your goals. This is ultraimportant. Whatever you do and whatever your current circumstance, just don't forget to keep dreaming. Use that imagination of yours to visualize your life the way you want it because as I mentioned earlier—and you already know this—the life you desire already exists in a parallel reality. By focusing on it, you pull that existing reality toward you. Don't resent your current job, boss, spouse, residence, friends, or family. Don't cling to them either! One thing to keep in mind is that whoever is currently supporting you is a *conveyer*, not a *provider*. Don't fret anything or anyone because the only real provider is *God*. Your boss or whoever is supplying you a sum of money to support yourself is merely God's conveyer. Remember that the universe is always subsidizing us or teaching us lessons through other people as well. People are merely angels, mediators, and conveyers but *not* providers. The source of your economy is the universe, not another person or organization. Don't resent your boss, your spouse, your parents, or the government, because they aren't the real source of your income. When you reform your belief patterns and mainly focus on what you want your life to become, all you have to do next is acknowledge how it's already a guaranteed reality for you, release your desires to the universe, keep calm, and prepare to be surprised. You might lose your job just as you were asking God for a promotion at work. If this is so, it might be because you need to clear the space for a new, more lucrative, and promising job to enter your life. It's important to be flexible enough to receive your blessings in different forms. Many times the object of our desire will not show up in the exact same form as we visualize it. Be willing to receive it in whichever form God knows will suit you best. Stay open-minded, and you'll receive your next *paycheck* just as you planned it or from where you least expect it.

THE WORLD NEEDS YOUR GIFT

Sometimes we sail through life with ease and stability; other times we may hit a bump and decide to reinvent ourselves, and yet other times we come to a halt without clear direction. Whichever one of these is your case, never forget that you have a gift, and that gift is your biggest contribution to the world. A personal contribution is basically a talent. Your talents are your generous gifts. Talents aren't always of an artistic, athletic, or entrepreneurial nature. If you can put a smile on someone else's face, that's talented enough. Find out what puts a smile on your own face, and you will have found your passion. I always encourage people to never stop exploring new ideas, activities, creative outlets, and interests.

Stay curious to your own likings and inclinations. I suggest you always sign yourself up to learn new skills, new languages, new sports, and new hobbies. Sometimes you have an affinity for something you don't even know yet because you don't expose yourself to new aptitudes. Other times you find out that what you wanted so bad is not attractive to you anymore. Your aspirations and offerings to the world keep shifting all the time. Sometimes we discover that we no longer have a passion for something, and we become interested in other things. This is no accident, and you must attune to the callings of your heart. Shifting from one desire to another is influenced by what the universe needs and stops needing from you at any given point in time. This is determined by the needs of the entire collective consciousness. We are all spiritually connected, given we all come from the same energetic source. This is how we are part of a collective consciousness. Whatever I do now affects not only my own life but creates a ripple effect across the universe as well that marks the lives of every vibrating being in our cosmos. There's a collective interest that wants you to do well because when you succeed, the entire universe benefits from it. Your talents suit every soul in the universe. Every desire of your heart is planted in you to serve not only your purpose but the collective consciousness as a whole. This is why you should never doubt that your desires are already granted. Longing for them is the biggest sign that they have been approved by the entire spiritual realm, which is betting on your courage to make them happen.

To get a better understanding of our collective consciousness, we can analyze it from nature's perspective. They say natural disasters are simply expressions of an accumulated, negative collective consciousness. The ripple effect is there doing its job. Mother Earth obeys the energetic makeup of our collective minds and actions. Nature mirrors back at us what we carry within too. Don't think for a second that only people act as our mirrors. The environment reflects back at us what we are made of and what we carry within as well. You are as perfect, gorgeous, and breathtaking as nature. Let's think of ourselves as those trees that stand strong, abundant, fruitful, and stunning. The universe generously provides them with light and water without having them struggle at all. They grow, bloom, and shed in perfect harmony with the seasons without ever challenging their natural cycles. They don't worry about receiving. They just *give*. They give us their beauty for all to admire and give us their shade for all to sit under. They give animals shelter and give out oxygen for all to breathe. It doesn't get more generous than that! They don't beg the sun for sunlight or have anxiety attacks, wondering if the rain will shower them soon. They don't bribe the earth to be able to plant their seeds in its soil, and they certainly don't feel threatened by all the other surrounding trees standing tall and strong. The trees understand that the universe has enough soil, space, sunlight, and water for all of them. They are in surrender mode all the time, obeying the laws of the universe, so the universe provides for them effortlessly. The trees reflect back at us what we are made of, and this is why they are so awe-inspiring to our eyes.

When nature strikes with disaster, it is also showing us a side of our collective consciousness that is not too pretty. All the abusive, violent, dishonest, unjust, and cruel doings of human beings accumulate until there comes a point when this overload of negativity looks for an outlet. It must express itself somewhere because energy doesn't just disappear into nothingness; it has to go somewhere. Every conscious act has a collective ripple effect that obeys the law of cause and effect, remember? So we get earthquakes, tsunamis, hurricanes, wildfires, blizzards, floods, avalanches, droughts, and heat waves that take lives, destroy homes, and break our hearts. Nature is perfectly mirroring back at us not only all of our strengths but also all of our weaknesses simultaneously, so be like the astonishing trees that stand glorious, generous, loving, and trusting. It is a much easier and prosperous way of life!

GENEROUS GAIA

Nature is very healing. We count on Mother Earth to take away our negative energy load and transmute it to positive energy because this is exactly what it does. It cradles us, feeds us, warms us up, and inspires us. Nature can also smash, starve, freeze, and scare us, but when it does, it does it with a purpose to change us for the better. How many times have we gotten a wake-up call or a change of attitude or had to embark on a new beginning after a natural disaster? No natural occurrence is in vain, and Mother Nature is very wise. This earth we live on is so generous that it literally takes the blows for us. Earth saves us from ourselves. When we go out for a walk, swim in the ocean, hike a mountain, or lean on a tree, Mother Nature pays attention and feels into our energy with an inclination to balance it out. Whatever negativity we carry, it takes it from us and cleanses us out so that we can gain clarity and inner peace. Our contact with nature can become much more significant if we visit her with an intention to heal.

Sometimes we feel so out of it, so blue, so down, and we have no idea why or how to get rid of it. Whether you realize it or not, relating to people can either feed your good energy or drain you of it, depending on the vibe of those you come into contact with. This is why it's so important to surround yourself with people you admire and aspire to become. People who offer good advice and who talk with optimism and are encouraging and admirable are the ones you want to call your friends and family. You will know who these people are by the way they live, the type of relation-ships they have, their finances, and the way you feel when you are in their presence. People who drain you of your good energy are those who talk about conflicts and love to gossip—who constantly struggle and engage in self-destructive behaviors. You can spot energy suckers in those who say they are happy for you, but your instinct can read that they are rather envious because they live in a state of lack and mental misery all the time. Being around them feels like a cloud of despair, and suddenly feelings of sadness and darkness take over you. Sometimes these people are people we love and want to help or make them good company, but we must be wise enough to protect our energy when these loved ones refuse to make a change in their attitudes, beliefs, behaviors, or lifestyles. Many times the friends we hang out with, the people we date, or those we spend the most time with end up defining us because people's energy rubs off on us. Before we know it, we begin to talk, act, and think like them whether we notice it or not.

Some people can't seem to make significant life changes for the better and then wonder why. They complain and seek advice from their friends when they feel depressed, but their own friends are stuck in a rut. They talk to their family members about their despair, but their own family members have mediocre perspectives on life and advise them fallaciously or ignore them altogether. Misery loves company, and sometimes those we love the most are stuck in negative attitudes, habits, and behaviors. We must make an effort to avoid that negativity and become more selective of whom we decide to share our energy with. We were born to become the best version of ourselves, not to stagnate. Mother Nature is always ready to remind us of our true nature and to cleanse our energy when it gets plagued with negativity. We belong to the earth, and it will make sure to nurture us the most when we can't find nourishment elsewhere.

It is important to find nourishment in positive relationships, passion-ate professions, healthy diets, and a positive attitude, but don't hesitate to look for solace out in nature as well. Nature offers to channel out all nega-tivity that doesn't serve you in moving forward. The energy of the earth is so mighty, powerful, and abundant with a purpose. Its main purpose is to heal and balance everything that inhabits it because it is in its best interest that you and I survive since our life is what makes it throb. When things go wrong, it only reflects our resistance to the natural cycles that Mother Nature intends for us. We can get so out of touch with her, but this doesn't have to be so if we just get back with its flow and become mindful of its healing energy. We receive the best parenting and nourishment from Mother Nature, which equips us with all we need to live a long and healthful life, but it also scolds us if we need a wake-up call, an epiphany, or a situation that helps us learn new lessons to become wiser and stronger. It is true that our Mother Earth wants only the fittest to walk on it, which is why it is always trying to make us stronger. If we learn to identify with and respect the patterns and strengths of nature and find nourishment in her, we will thrive like the trees that grow strong and regal, like the ocean that is powerfully abundant, and like the rivers that freely flow through obstacles and barriers and find their path effortlessly.

We don't have to suffer in our negativity because Mother Earth is always willing to take the punches for us. Her only condition is that we allow ourselves to acknowledge all our accumulated resentments before handing them over to her to be transmuted to light and love. Natural disasters are manifestations of our built-up rage and fears. The earth recycles our pain and makes it better this way, and we aren't always meant to be in nature's catastrophic way, just like we aren't always meant to be flying in a crashing plane. Energy, both good and bad, has to go somewhere, and the bad energy can't just stagnate or magically disappear. Mother Nature offers us one of many ways to rid ourselves of this dense negativity to avoid getting hurt. When we carry unexpressed hate, anger, sadness, or hostility, it will always look to create an impact somehow because energy needs an outlet. Either we get sick or break bones if it impacts our bodies, or we break things, drive our vehicles into accidents, engage in violent acts, or position ourselves in destructive situations. Negative energy wants to destroy; positive energy wants to create. The beauty about negative energy is that it wants to destroy old patterns that don't serve you. Negative energy is not your enemy; it is your guide and compass. Every time you feel rage or despair, become still and bring it to your awareness, acknowledge that it doesn't serve you, bless it, and release it. We are beings of light and can't afford darkness to come dim us out. In the game of life, our sole purpose is to keep shining bright, so learning how to handle darkness wisely is our most powerful skill.

It is in nature's best interest that we stay positive, so get out and get purified as often as you need. Dig your feet deep in the sand, swim in the lake, sun gaze, walk barefoot on the grass, hug a tree, and kiss the ground you walk on, and when you do, imagine all your heavy burdens melt away as the force of nature envelopes you in white light that cleanses your soul of all negative excess baggage. Do you remember the movie *Forest Gump* when the angry and hopeless lieutenant Dan is healed and transformed after coming face-to-face with God in the midst of a hurricane? He lost his legs in a battle and had blocking beliefs about his destiny that didn't allow him to live a fulfilling life. When he was ready to acknowledge and surrender his fury, God sent him a powerful storm that drove him to fully express his outrage. Strapped to a boat's mast, he cursed and challenged God in the middle of the storm in what turned out to be the most cathartic experience of his life. It was as if the hurricane took all his rage with it so that he didn't have to swim in it anymore, and it cleansed his spirit. He came out a new man after this face-off with nature. The storm was symbolic of Lieutenant Dan's anger, and when he called God out for answers, God gave him relief through that hurricane. Mother Nature is packed with relief. It wants to channel our negative load and make our spirits better. Don't just bask in the glory of nature, but feed your body from it too! Just like a woman's breast milk is the optimal food for her baby, the fruits of the earth are the optimal food meant to heal and nourish us too.

GRATEFULNESS

ATTITUDE OF GRATITUDE

People do not feel grateful because of their happiness but rather feel happy because they are grateful. Look around yourself, and activate your abundant self. Your glass is always half full! It is easy to feel grateful for the great things in life, but real character comes from feeling appreciative of the negative ones too. When you thank God for the challenges and face every obstacle with a positive attitude, you become the captain of your own ship. Being positive in a negative situation is not naïve; it is leadership. All adversity is an opportunity in disguise. Every bump on the road is just trying to center us back to our true loving nature from where all good fortune and happiness emanate. Our mishaps are nothing more than blessings that we must handle with emotional intelligence and use to our benefit. You can hack your depression, disease, and hostility with "thank-you pills." The cards you are currently being dealt have two sides only: a black side and a white side. Everything in life comes with pros and cons; there's no escaping this. The happiest people out there have plenty of things to complain about, but they don't waste their energy focusing on the dark side of their cards because they know that their energy is what fuels their focus. The most depressive people out there also have plenty of things to feel blessed about, but their focus is completely fixed on the dark. We will always have psychological blocks to work on so that we can learn to love deeply again, and gratitude is one of the most powerful tools to help us break free from the chains of our subconscious mind. Your troubles are meant to center you, not throw you off into depression, loathing, and self-destruction. Finding your passions and using them as a life compass is easy; acknowledging your blessings when everything is going well is effortless, but using your troubles to bring you back to your loving essence is not always a walk in the park. To benefit from your misfortunes, you must use gratitude.

Gratefulness can sometimes be clouded by fear. How can we be grateful for something or someone when all they pose is a huge threat? How can we feel appreciative of others if they humiliate, judge, abandon, betray, ignore, or hurt us? How can we enjoy the company of a person who makes us feel trapped or stuck? Instead of fearing these people, have you considered trusting the role that they're playing in your life? What if they represent a repressed side of your personality that you neglect and refuse to work on? What if their participation in your life is literally serving you instead of wounding you? Could you trust that your abusive spouse, demanding parents, or aloof children are simply trying to teach you to develop more love, forgiveness, and optimism? Sometimes when all we do is focus on the things that aren't going well or focus on the flaws of others, we can't help but become magnets of more of that negativity. Our energy obeys our perception so flawlessly that everything we focus on in ourselves or in others will keep manifesting until we shift our lens. Gratefulness is a magnificent lens shifter. When we see life through a gratitude lens, everything starts to make sense and transform before our eyes. All of a sudden, you are compelled to act based on trust instead of fear because you realize that everything and everyone are serving you, not threatening you. Nobody is in your way, no one is keeping you from living the life you desire, and no one is holding you back from happiness; it's all a product of your fear-based thoughts. When you feel grateful for the role others are playing in your life, let their defects go, and start focusing on just feeling happy in spite of everyone, you will become a magician. It won't matter how much money is in your bank account, what you look like, where you live, what your family says or does, or what is your relationship status. It won't matter anymore, because the magician in you will start to magically attract blessing into your life. Your magic wand will touch everyone's hearts, and you will experience the unimaginable. You'll get a phone call, a job opportunity, or a travel gift; make a new friend; be introduced to a new social circle; and so on. In other words, you'll bump into a variety of people or circumstances that match your new and improved high frequency of gratitude.

Focusing on your blessings and what you have going for you right now is powerful enough to manifest all that you want. It's all based on your frequency. Feeling grateful floods you with white light. If you are charged with trusting, grateful, positive energy, it will propel you to amazing heights. If your energy is fear based, paranoid, and self-defeating, your low frequency will keep you stagnant. It's best to adopt an attitude of gratitude. That person who threatens to come between you and your partner? You can be thankful for him or her. The economy crisis that threatens to sweep away your savings? You can be thankful for that too. The boss who threatens to fire you? Thank him or her. Be thankful not just for the good but also for the inconvenient because what seems inconvenient now is there to make things better, believe it or not. Things won't always go the way you want, and this is normal because you can't see the bigger picture with your five senses. You must trust that there is a divine plan throwing things at you to improve your life in ways you can't fathom right now. Go with the flow, and surrender into the waves of life. Change is constant; we can't control that. By feeling grateful for life's ups and downs, we welcome huge blessings into our lives. It often happens that we look back and realize that we wouldn't have had our experience happen in any other way because certain setbacks made us better people or allowed for other great things to enter our lives. Absolutely no big achievement or joy in life came without obstacles of some sort. You must discipline your disappointment and learn how to keep a positive outlook because whatever is troubling you is helping you build character. Whatever is rattling you is just there to test your faith. You are going to focus on all the blessings you currently have, and you will train yourself to keep a grateful and trusting mind-set before any setback. Your mind should stay focused on your goals of love, success, unity, and peace and ignore the threat that any adversity poses. Rely on the things that you do have, lean on your loved ones, and always anticipate the sun that comes out after every thunderstorm because it always does.

Base your decisions on trust instead of fear. Strengthen your perception of safety. Notice the way you feel around people. Your energy is telling you something. We can learn to work with the vibes we get as we walk through life and use them to our benefit. We ought to train ourselves to become great energy manipulators! If, for instance, another person makes us feel tense, we can practice taming that tension by acknowledging that the other person poses absolutely no threat in our lives, and this way of thinking will transform the tension into confidence and ease. This positive energy is what our magic wands are made of. There are absolutely no threats out there. Threats live in our minds only. When you ease yourself into riding the waves of life, allow yourself to mingle with different types of people, learn to coexist with nagging family members, explore new atmospheres, and be open-minded to new ideas, you will learn how to use the innate ability you were born with to tackle your personal resistance. Sometimes we resist living because we are so afraid, but we can always recenter by reminding ourselves that there is only now and now is safe. Be grateful for right now.

It's human nature to fall back into negativity and self-defeating thoughts, so don't punish yourself for stumbling. The key is to catch yourself drifting and pull yourself back to your source. The biggest sign that you are distancing yourself from your center is when you feel like you want to complain, because complaining comes from a place of feeling undervalued or unloved, which are both lies. Complaining is nothing more than an impulsive expression of lies that is charged with fear-based emotions. Complaining displays our insecurities and loves to blame others. It only ends up fueling guilt and shame because as you display how ungrateful and insecure you feel, you may hurt others. The things you complain about may be unfair to the person you attack. Catching yourself when you get an impulse to complain could save you from a verbal hangover. It is our egos that love to complain. The ego is the one that focuses on what's missing, what's hurting, or what's unfortunate. If we allow ego to take the driver's seat, its fears and complaints will eventually collide us into conflictive situations. Let gratitude drive instead. It's a real life saver.

YOUR PURCHASE POWER

Every achievement comes with a price. The bigger the goal, the higher the price. We purchase our goals with our energy, and the higher our energy, the more it can afford. Since you are fundamentally nothing more than a big bundle of energy, think of yourself as a hefty bank account. How much are you worth? In essence, we were all born with the same purchase power, but each of us has been spending our energy in different ways. Some have been investing energy wisely, while others have been spending energy on things that aren't worth it. If you think of yourself as a big bank account and your money is in the form of throbbing energy, imagine that every self-defeating thought that you allow to enter your mind and every self-destructive action you engage in are like thieves who snatch a big chunk of your funds. Your energy thieves are worry, fear, envy, greed, hate, remorse, guilt, shame, robbing, cheating, hurting, numbing, insulting, cursing, and lying. Your energy is your economy, and you want it to have big purchasing power, so spend your energy wisely.

Watch out for energy vampires too! They suck the energy out of you when you're weak, vulnerable, guilt-ridden, and full of fear. To shield yourself against them, make sure to focus on the positive side of things, trust that nobody has the power to hurt you but yourself, and sail through life with an appreciation lens. Energy vampires don't just come in the form of people but also in the form of drugs and other addictive substances.

These lure you into making senseless choices. Somebody once told me, "Oh, come on! But you gotta live a little!" I thought, "Yes. Live. This is why I'd rather stay away from them, because they snatch the life out of me!" It all boils down to personal choice, and I'm not judging anyone for their choices because all choices are perfect. Perfection is relative to each person's goals and how they manage to balance their lives out. My only aim here is to explain how energy expenditure works so that you have a broader sense of what you are capable of and you can protect your energy like you protect your finances. Have you ever heard that a person's financial situation reflects his or her belief patterns and that positive energy attracts abundance? It's true! Some people talk about protecting their energy by visualizing a shielding white light encapsulating their bodies, but it goes way beyond just locking yourself up in an imaginary white bubble of light. The white light won't fully protect you if you still believe that you are surrounded by bad people, threatening situations, and negative vibes. In truth, the white light protecting you from harm is everywhere around you, and you activate it when you realize there is no threat and only blessings in your everyday encounters.

THE OVERANALYZING TRAP

Keep it simple. The whole idea of focusing on your blessings and distancing yourself from a fear-based mentality does not mean that you have to strive for perfection. Nobody is grading you or keeping score. You're still a human being bound to make mistakes, and this is part of your learning experience. Don't try to overanalyze yourself. I once fell into this trap, and it feels just as self-defeating as worrying and resenting do. Overanalyzing leads to disapproving of every stumble you have as you strive for perfection. Wanting to be perfect is also unfair to your naturally human duality. All you have to do is stay mindful and try your best to treat yourself with kindness and love. It suffices to pick yourself back up as soon as you fall and feel proud of standing back up instead of feeling disappointed that you fell. To feel disappointed of your failed attempts is a way to punish yourself because you basically tell yourself you aren't good enough. You must be very careful of your self-talk because whatever you tell yourself, you are telling the universe. The universe wants to hear self-empowering, optimistic, and compassionate comments so that it can give you back more of the same!

Don't break your head trying to decipher every single detail of the origin of your mistakes, fears, and preoccupations. All you have to be aware of is how you feel now and use all the tools I've talked about in this book to pick your mood back up. A part of being kind to yourself is granting your soul the time it needs to heal its wounds and pick up new habits. Expecting yourself to be perfectly recovered from all your blockages over-night is unrealistic and unfair. "But you said time doesn't exist and that everything happens now!" I just laughed to myself writing this because I am so analytic, and this is a remark I'd throw at anybody preaching these things to me, but I do have an answer. Remember that chapter I wrote on forgiveness? Being patient and kind with yourself when you fail is the equivalent of forgiving yourself. Everything happens in this very moment, true, so if you stumble right now and forgive yourself for it right now, you will also succeed right now. A useful thing to remember is that no matter how many times you fail, the universe will keep presenting new opportu-nities for you to succeed because the universe is relentless to ensure that you reach your desired goals and dreams.

Don't try to figure out exactly where people come from. Don't focus on their motives. Don't delve on the past trying to decipher the origin of your weaknesses so much that you exhaust yourself. Don't try to come up with a soap opera in your head made up of enemies, a damsel in distress, a climax, and a happy ending. These things are irrelevant to your happiness in the long run. If we had it our way, we'd know it all because we are natu-rally curious cats, but learning people's motives or even your own motives won't pull you out of your darkness. All that matters is that you feel good now. This is what I call the "path of higher awareness and least effort." Stay present, and notice where your focus is. If your focus is relapsing to the past or speeding up to the future and this is feeding your worries, guilt, shame, or anxiety, it's time to suspend all the obsession. Focus on this very moment where everything is joyful and comforting in spite of what is going on around you. You have that joy and comfort in your heart and those rose-colored lenses in your pocket, so pull them out, put them on, and start seeing life through the pink lens.

You need good, clean, vibrating energy to deal with any crisis just as you need your savings account to rescue you in an emergency. You bet-ter believe that this game called life comes with its fair share of crises, so I'm just advising you to be prepared. Keep your energy in check. The secret to the pursuit of happiness is not in chasing what you want but rather elevating your game frequency until what you want pursues you. The universe has a way of aligning you with people, things, and situations that match the energy you put out. The more you improve yourself and raise your vibration, the more you will see things that add to your joy and benefit your well-being.

In a nutshell, overanalyzing leads to impulsive actions that lead to remorseful damage. If, after reading all this, you still wonder what the point of feeling grateful is since you still wish you were living a different life, I'd remind you that loving this life of yours is the answer. The desire to escape your current life is simply because there is something about it that hurts really bad. You are simply trying to run away from your own pain. Surrendering to your life and learning to face the fears and sadness it presents you with is the key to your freedom. This is the path of higher awareness and least effort. One of the best lessons you can learn in life is to master how to remain calm in the face of adversity and figure out how all your pain is serving you to make you stronger, wiser, and more loving.

Learning to love the person you live with, the city you reside in, the company you work for, the friends you talk to, and the property you live in is the answer to all your prayers. Facing your life courageously without wanting to run away from it will provide you with a huge epiphany that will mend every conflict, dissolve all your sadness, and miraculously transform your life before your eyes. The things that now bother you will never go away unless you learn to embrace them fully. Once again, keep in mind that I'm referring to life situations that don't threaten your existence or your dignity. There are times when you must eject yourself from abusive circumstances or relationships that can potentially destroy you. In these cases, you must run for help to save your life. Trust me; when it's time to go, you will know it's time to go. You won't have another option. There will be no question or inner conflict acting like a tug of war of "Should I stay or should I go?" In these life-threatening events, you would not be escaping; you would be saving your life. Relevant to my case in point, I am referring to the remaining majority of the situations where you just feel miserably stuck because the grass always seems greener on the other side and you beat yourself up for the way your life is going. In these instances, the person, place, or thing that makes you feel hopelessly out of place is indirectly trying to teach you something beautiful, and all you want to do is run the opposite way. You can very well run, but I guarantee that you will bump into the same fear and sadness elsewhere because life has a way of placing you in front of your grief until you hurt no more. Don't overanalyze where you come from or where you're going. Surrender to this moment; feel grateful for the opportunities it is presenting you with to forgive, love, and embrace; and let the universe work its magic.

TRUST WHAT YOU ARE GRATEFUL FOR

Feeling grateful for your life means you feel grateful for every single person who plays a part in it too. There are no exceptions to this aphorism. You can't feel grateful and simultaneously have an aversion for someone. Many times we suspect or keep a distance from certain people because we say we can't trust them, but gratefulness comes with assurance. You feel grateful for people because you trust that they are meant to support your journey, not dismantle it. To really feel gratitude in your heart, you must yank out all disdain from it because embracing and trusting people mean you trust your life's process. Trust the ex-spouses, the in-laws, partners, significant others, coworkers, boss, family, and friends, but don't trust them while you hold on to fear. If you just tell yourself you'll trust them but feel paranoid that they will conspire against you, don't be surprised if they do. Surrender your fear, and learn to trust from a place of faith and love. Know that divine love is forever looking after you in a way that nothing anyone does poses a threat. You are being protected by a higher power, and everyone is meant to walk beside you in your journey. Nobody is on a mission to harm or betray you until you believe they are. This is how powerful your thoughts are. Your certainty has the capacity to inspire others to do you wrong and then you'll tell yourself, "I knew that person was evil." You're the one who fueled their betrayal with your negative conviction. I assure you; you can ease down and enjoy the ride by trusting others. Feel grateful for them, and visualize halos over their heads. Don't fish for clues. Don't doubt your loved ones or your acquaintances. Genuinely believe they are there to support you in anything and everything. If life needs you to know something about them, this information will come to you effortlessly. You don't need to spy on people, you don't need to eavesdrop, and you don't need to doubt. Those who seek shall find, so try to fish for good things only. Trusting will soothe and relieve you, as it will inspire others to trust you too. You attract what you are.

If someone does betray you while you were fully trusting them, it just means life has different plans for you and it's time to move on. This is part of the inevitable. There are things in life we can't control. If a stab in the back was a case of the inevitable, just be thankful for the person's brief participation in your life. Be grateful for whatever lessons they brought to the table, and bless them away on their ensuing journey. It might bring you hurt and disappointment, but don't hold grudges. If they were going to betray you, they were going to do it with or without your trust, and it's better they did while you trusted them so that their departure leaves you with a clear conscience. You believed in them, so in the end you had nothing to do with it. It had to happen. What scars us is when we feel like we provoked their disloyalty. You don't need to be marked like that. Doubting people drains us of so much precious energy that is not worth spending when you attempt to control the inevitable. A painful occurrence like this is also a blessing in disguise. You will prove and comprehend it later. Just be thankful and keep loving because love is the one thing you have an unlimited supply of.

Gratitude is a powerful virtue that can also help you shift your tendency of avoiding others to trusting them. I used to avoid so many individuals until I learned that they would keep hunting me unless I embraced their existence. I used to feel that people were hard to trust, so it felt safer to be a loner. I would make up stories in my head of how they were after me, how they were superficial, and how all they wanted was something from me or to judge me and to act as a friend only to study me and then go off to gossip about me. Ask me if these things ever happened. Most of the time, they were all outlandish assumptions I made up in my mind. My insecurities from the past loved to construct these ideas and conspiracy theories that just made me dread people. I became such a hermit because it took me a while to understand that most people out there were not trying to do anything other than get to know me and share things in common. I even had a hard time relaxing into social situations because I was always defensive with my sense of perfection. Deep inside I feared that not looking, acting, talking, or standing perfectly would be reason enough for others to lose interest in me. It was energy draining to be so conscious of what I'd wear, what I'd talk about, how I'd react, what I would share with people and what I'd choose to keep to myself, how I'd present myself, and what I'd do if left alone. Oh, the anxiety of having no one to talk to! It was almost like I never really learned to be social because I was always sipping on a cocktail that gave me liquid courage. The ironic part is that even the drink never brought out my true colors. Nobody, let alone myself, knew who I really was because for years I was numbing my fear of rejection. When I finally decided to change my life around, I used gratefulness to save me from myself. I started focusing on all the blessings that others brought into my life. I thought of them as angels sent from heaven to shower me with ideas, support, and kindness. Many triggers would make me defensive with others. I knew my triggers were activated when I started to feel shaky or like I wanted to go home, but I learned to spot those triggers and use them for my own good. I used every trigger to practice feeling grateful for the opportunity to rise and overcome.

You can feel grateful for everyone, even for the people who aren't the nicest to you. You can shower them with loving thoughts in your head, and you will surprise yourself when their approach to you changes. When you feel grateful for another person, you radiate a white light that he or she naturally responds to with the same kindness and respect that you hold for that person. The person won't even know what hit him or her when his or her heart calms down after you focus on what is good about his or her existence. Every single viewpoint we hold of another human being has an equally opposite stance that we can choose to focus on. Instead of believing "My boss is such a perfectionist prick who holds impossible standards, and no one can stand him," opt for the thought "My boss is such a perfectionist, which has allowed him outstanding success for his company, and I am grateful to be part of his organization that has me learning something new every day; thanks to the high standards that are always held in that work space." You have the choice; you always have that choice. You decide how to react. You decide whether to trust or be paranoid, whether to thank or to curse. Gratitude equals blessings.

SETTING BOUNDARIES

A thing that's worth mentioning before we try to become all saintly and holier-than-thou pedants is that at the end of the day, we must not give in to people or circumstances that compromise our health or dignity. To set boundaries is not a selfish thing to do; it's simply smart and self-respecting. Yes, when people annoy us, it can be best to develop compassion and tolerance *unless* they begin to disrespect us. I would advise you to stand your ground until they learn to treat you decently. The whole thing with trusting and being compassionate, grateful, and forgiving is to not fall into the trap of letting others take advantage of you. There is a fine line between being grateful and being naïve. You still want to be regarded as a person of character who knows how to stand up for yourself and for what's right. Focusing on what's good does not mean you will allow others to step all over you as you carry on unaffected. The whole idea is to not fall short like those who love to complain, blame, curse, and disrespect. Sometimes we do have to call out people on their blunders to let them know that we won't be the Dumpster for their garbage, but there is an art to defending yourself in a dignified way. The key is to tame your emotions before you take action because in the end you might have to distance yourself from the person or warn him or her of what's acceptable and what's unacceptable to give him or her an opportunity to reconsider and modify his or her behavior around you. When setting boundaries, you need to make sure you cool off first because many of us have made the terrible mistake of reacting to an insulting behavior with disrespectful words, insults, and fear-based impulses that are hard to row back from. I once had a friend warn me about this, but I never paid much attention, so I had to learn this the hard way. It's perfectly acceptable to freak out and lose your temper with another person's behavior or words because we are human. What will set you apart from the rest of your equals is the way you handle your emotions. To set boundaries is essential when it comes to building character and having others respect you the way you deserve.

A valuable thing I learned is that there's a right timing for setting boundaries too. When you find yourself in a quarrel and you feel a line was crossed, remember this golden word: "downtime." Before you start giving out ultimatums, making demands, scolding, and threatening others, it is much better to contain yourself, leave if you have to leave, and take time to dissect your feelings before you confront people. Sometimes people don't mean any harm, and we misinterpret things. Other times people just try to address an issue we have a hard time facing, so we find it easier to take offense. And yet other times people are, indeed, straight up demeaning, and we have every right to protest and put our foot down. Whichever the case, it is best we take our fiery feelings next door, even if for five minutes, just to let them cool down before we shoot them back out. When we are charged up with emotion, it is very common for our inner firecracker to fully convince us that whatever we are feeling and thinking is absolutely righteous and has to be told right this instant! This is part of the irrational impulsiveness you want to avoid for your own good. If you feel anxious to speak out, your very anxiety is the biggest sign that it's not time to reprimand just yet. Discipline your disappointment before you go out to say something that can be hard to take back. Your zealous initiative could backfire. Who wants that? Been there, done that. It's a guilt- and shame-fueled ride that can last days, months, and even years. Avoid it! Only after you've digested your feelings and cooled down, it is best to converse with the person in a place where you have the privacy and time to do so. You most definitely don't want other people prying into your sensitive issues. Keeping these matters just between the both of you shows maturity and respect for yourself and for the other person as well. Many times you will find out that your arguments are magnified in the moment, and there are practically no boundaries to set. We have to admit that we humans are complex beings, and sometimes our hormones, accumulated stress, over-analyzing, and lack of rest take over, and we blow up for nothing only to apologize the day after. Don't set boundaries on impulse. When you set unnecessary boundaries, you risk making others feel inappropriate, and this can hurt more in the long run. Controlling yourself in the midst of discussions is imperative.

WE NEED EACH OTHER

There is as much healing power and self-discovery in relating to others as there is in solitude and meditation. Isolated comfort zones are misleading, as we can convince ourselves with pride that we live in isolation because we are independent, sensitive beings who need own space for introspection and inspiration. We tell others that we don't need to be surrounded by anyone because we aren't needy or reliant and that we value our own space. This mentality denotes resistance. I've been guilty as charged of using this train of thought to justify my fear of relating. This attitude displays a bundle of associated symptoms, such as not trusting others; low self-esteem; fear of being judged; overachieving to feel worthy; lack of intimacy as a by-product of guarding one's vulnerability; and a trapped inner child desperately crying for attention, love, and acknowledgment.

Many celebrities out there make it to the pinnacle of fame and fortune in their ambitious quest for love and acceptance only to reach the top and realize that all the love they sought is not found in those heights. Nobody ever reminded them that it was found within. They never had proper guidance to help them tap back into their source, where all the healing, peace, and affection overflow. So what happened next? Their voids got even deeper, the Band-Aids that covered their wounds eventually fell off, and they found themselves feeling so exposed, hurting, and unprotected that they used their wealth and fortune to build great fortresses to hide in.

They thought stardom and recognition would give them the acceptance and care they always longed for, only to realize that love is not found in superficial places. Tragically, as their mistrust and vulnerability multiplied, many of them found solace in destructive habits and not on supportive people, and the inevitable came to be. We wake up to a news headline of yet another celebrity found dead in a shiny castle.

Reaching out to people when we begin to stagnate can help us move our energy around so that we can activate our lives again. It may seem scary at first because calling others and making an effort to interact mean dragging ourselves out of our safe cocoons. "But I am so perfect in here! Have them come visit me instead!" That defeats the purpose; trust me. Life is full of surprises, opportunities, wake-up calls, creative stimuli, and dynamism out there. The best motive for someone to come visit you in a case like this is to strap some shoes on your feet and take you out for a stroll, a ride, or even a flight. Talking to people also helps to show you what you've been bottling up inside. Repressed feelings and ideas eat up at you little by little and dim your light. Counselors and life coaches can be overrated, but I promise you these people are not meant to heal you. They are meant to listen for you to heal yourself as you expose what you've been hiding for so long. Expelling what you've dug in the dark for so many years can be so cathartic, you have no idea. This could be the only treatment you need to overcome your heaviest burdens.

If investing on a counselor is not an option, then open up to your loved ones. You can't imagine how many family members have absolutely no clue of what their relatives are sometimes going through. Sometimes we know so damn well how to cover up our grief and despair that we could win Academy Awards for acting so wholesome, when in truth we feel broken. Sometimes we are afraid to worry our loved ones or find it pointless to spill out our sentiments because we figure that they won't have the answers or solutions we seek. Remember they are not meant to shower you with solutions because you're damn right; they don't have any. You carry your own answers within. Sometimes all we need is other people's empathy and warmth. Sometimes our biggest relief is when others embrace us, pat us on the back, and tell us everything will be all right.

Expecting them to plan a course of action to tackle our problems is not what we're after, and we know this. This is why we feel hesitant to reach out to them. We don't trust that their affection alone can heal us, but I'm here to assure you, there's no better medicine than that. Love and embrace are the antidotes. People heal us this way.

You don't always have to be surrounded by loving family members and childhood friends to feel this love. Challenge yourself to explore the world around you. There are potential family members in all the new people we meet along the way. Family is not established on paper or solely in your DNA makeup. We choose our families, as they are born in our hearts. You are never alone, even when you feel you are. All you have to do is get out there and connect a little. It may feel overwhelming at first, but the rewards are amazing when you take an initiative. Look for support groups or voluntary programs in your community that offer a safe space to share your truth. Embracing the truth is pivotal to recover from adversity or disheartenment. Find a place where they foster a safe environment for people to open up. Sharing things about yourself gives you amazing confidence, as you get to release every blocked emotion that had been manipulating you on a subconscious level. On the other hand, listening to other people's stories can inspire you in ways you don't even imagine too. It can help take the focus off yourself, which helps tremendously to gather your thoughts later and evaluate your situation from a different angle. There is something highly therapeutic and sacred in sharing your truth with others. Strangers can become friends who share similar backgrounds, experiences, and emotions. Other people you thought you had nothing in common with may end up becoming a very special part of your walk of life. God has never abandoned us and never will. This is true. But it is also true that God wants to reach out to you through others, so locking yourself up can be more dangerous than getting out. Believe this! You won't have a series of private epiphanies in the comfort of your living room for the rest of your life. People are angels, messengers, supporters, brothers, and sisters, so be *grateful* for them, get out, and *bond*.

GRATITUDE PRAYER

Dear God,

Thank you for today. Thank you for my senses. Thank you for giving me a birthright and the power to reclaim what is mine. I am grateful for my free will and the marvelous things I can accomplish with it. Thank you for giving me a healing heart that can transmute everything to good and for making me autonomous to stand strong in spite of everything. Thank you for my creativity and imagination that show me what I'm capable of. Thank you for always standing by my side and showing up in the form of people, gifts, nature, opportunities, animals, and coincidental occurrences. I am grateful for my relationships that help me balance myself out and show me the meaning of life. I appreciate every beat of my heart, as it reminds me that you reside in it. I am receptive to your unlimited guidance, love, and wisdom, as I am certain you are my sole creator, provider, and guardian. As above, so below.

Amen.

YOU DECIDE

You decide who you want to be. At the end of the day, you are made of everything this life has to offer, and it's up to you how you want to carry out this eternal day. This is it. Today is all that's given to us. Whatever you choose to believe, how you choose to act, and what attitude you choose to adopt this morning is what will decide the things you'll manifest in your life. God has gifted us with a treasure chest made of free will, and it contains all possibilities. All possibilities are granted to you because you are essentially dual from birth. You're made of light and darkness simultaneously, which gives you the freedom to choose which side of the spectrum you will radiate from on right now. You decide if you will be loving or resentful, compassionate or judgmental, mindful or compulsive, responsible or blaming. You decide which lens you'll see through today because whatever you perceive out there in the world is nothing but a reflection of your perception. You are in charge. How lucky are you to be permanently surrounded by divine angels? All the people you interact with are angels sent from heaven. They're beings of light disguised in flesh and bone who have landed in your realm of perception to aid your spiritual evolution. Some of them will present a challenge to you and will push your buttons constantly, but they are all there with a perfect plan to benefit you and teach you how to love deeper, develop tolerance and compassion, surrender, forgive, and keep your faith in all that is good. How complex and dual are we that we sometimes confuse them for enemies or aggressors! It's time to open up our third eye and start blessing absolutely everything and everyone in our present reality. Get along with your peers, family, and strangers. See them for what they are. Remember that life won't change if you don't shift from within. You'll never control people's behavior, and nothing that anyone does will decide the outcome of your life, even if that's how it feels in this physical realm. Ultimately, you are the one moving the chess pieces around from a spiritual level. You are orchestrating everything to better suit your life purpose. Everything is happening to take you to a place where your state of joy is constantly flowing and attracting magnificent blessings and surprises into your life.

Dare to be selfish but only when selfish is righteous. Wanting love and abundance at someone else's expense is deceitful because what happens to another happens to you. If people do well, you do well. Life is only mirroring back at you the very concepts that live in your mind, so wish good upon everyone and spread the love. The only time you're allowed to be selfish is when another person's negativity tries to bring you down, in which case you don't need to approach that person at all. Misery loves company, and you have the right to walk away and send love from a distance. If people you love are gossiping, victimizing themselves, hurting others, or infusing you with dark vibes, you are wise to eject yourself from their negativity. Sharing bad judgment or justifying another person's pessimism to make him or her feel understood is absolutely irresponsible and detrimental to your own wellness. It is perfectly fair to be selfish by choosing not to participate in another person's loathing because it is up to you to protect your light. Your energy frequency depends only on you, and you can't afford to attract negativity just because someone you love needs you to identify with their unhappiness. You are meant to uplift people with good advice, not feed their cynicism. You are also meant to look after yourself, so if someone you love is not being receptive to your light, it's best to walk in another direction.

You are what you feel, and you feel what you know, so dive into as much self-knowledge as possible. If all you know is resentment, then you will resent, but if you know where resentment comes from and it helps you develop compassion, then you will know better, and you'll feel sympathy instead. To *know thyself* should be your biggest aim because you are so unique. The more you know about yourself, the freer and stronger you'll be. Finding happiness has nothing do with willpower and everything to do with knowledge because knowledge is power. Self-knowledge is all encompassing because what you learn and master in one area of life can be applied to many other experiences. Knowing yourself is also timeless because what you learn in this lifetime will benefit and support all your subsequent generations. Start tapping within! Never stop learning about yourself, about others, about life, and about the universe. Be like children who are always curious, receptive, trusting, and compassionate. The more wisdom you acquire, the more pain you will heal.

You'll never be done figuring this life out, and you'll always be a work in progress. Let go of deadlines and timelines to reach perfection or to conquer an issue. Treating disordered thinking and conduct is an ongoing thing. This is perfectly fine because ultimately, this is how it is meant to be! No one just figures things out one day and lives the rest of their lives free of conflict. Our energy constantly fluctuates from one side of the spectrum to another, and our job is to make it a habit to balance it out. There are many tools for this, including a healthy diet, meditation, positive thought patterns, forgiveness, exercise, and journaling, among others. To practice these healthy habits helps us tackle life's issues wisely and lovingly. Striving to do what is right is good enough because we will eventually fail, and what matters is to stand back up, not to be perfect. Perfection is not meant for human beings; it is meant for spirit only. Our souls are perfect indeed, but as long as we walk this earth, we are meant to stumble quite a few times. It is perfectly normal to lose our temper and get mad, sad, or depressed. What is *not* all right is to stay mad, sad, or depressed. We must learn how to bounce back to light to keep our frequency high as much as we can. This is what living is all about!

Focus on building a strong character instead of a perfect one. People with strong characters know how to control their emotions, express themselves with poise, and master standing back up when they stumble. They know the power of relationships and treat everyone with the same kindness and respect that we all deserve. They understand that we all come from different backgrounds, so they're tolerant and empathic. They allow themselves to feel everything because they know that facing their emotions is crucial to conquer personal blocks and evolve. They are integral in always trying to do what's right and may oftentimes be considered odd, but at least they'll be the odd ones in control who ooze quality and class.

Your heart knows best when it comes to how far you can go in life. You have a purpose, and the roads that lead to it are always clear because you have been sitting in the driver's seat the entire time. If you encounter roadblocks or dead ends, make U-turns and take alternate roads. What conflicts us the most is the picture we cling to of how life is supposed to be. We live thinking that our life has to go by XYZ, but this is not true. Life has a way of surprising you to remind you of how your mind is not in charge; only your spirit is. You can't consciously control what your spirit knows to be good for you. Your soul has already made a pact with the universe to take you down a path of perfect blessings and opportunity, but you won't be able to see this with your five senses. Surrendering to what is guarantees you great joy and inner peace. Don't question your life; don't complain. Just be grateful. The universe won't give you what you ask for because the universe does not hear what you are saying; it only feels the frequency of what you are feeling, so feel appreciative, content, and optimistic.

Whatever you do, I'll tell you right now one thing's for sure: You are meant to succeed in life and love; it's just a matter of time. There's no obstacle you can't overcome because you were born with the tools to fly high. Among the many tools out there, I have proven gratefulness, forgiveness, compassion, generosity, and faith to be the most effective. This is why I felt highly compelled to write this book. How could I not feel inspired to write about love's wonders? My heart never stops amazing me. It has taught me that wherever I am now is the perfect place to be. Love reminds me that no matter where I go, I've never left home because I carry home in my chest, and so do you.

www.ingramcontent.com/pod-product-compliance
Lightning Source LLC
Chambersburg PA
CBHW051833090426
42736CB00011B/1779